This is a work of fiction.
Any perceived error is either a flight-of-fancy
On the part of the author,
Or an oversight

For God's Sake

Soteriology

The Road To Redemption

By

Tony Sampson

Change no man's religion, change no man's politics, interrupt the sovereignty of no nation. Instead, teach man to use what he has and what he knows to the factual creation, within *any* political reference, a civilization on Earth for the first time.

L. Ron Hubbard

Prologue

Maggy

Six Months Earlier

I can't keep my eyes off my passenger. It's hard to believe I'm actually with my little brother. What a handsome man he's become. With that cute wave in his dark hair. And where did he get those broad shoulders? I'm sure I used to think of him as a runt.

Maybe it's inappropriate for a sister to be looking at her younger brother in this way, but I can easily rationalize seeing him with an admiring eye. What a wonderful husband he would be for some lucky woman. Except for the one unsolvable problem. He's a priest.

I haven't seen Tommy for five years. I was there, eight years ago, when he graduated from the School of Theology and soon thereafter at his ordination. Then it was two years later when he moved from a small mountain parish to preside over a church in Detroit. That was our last time together, until now.

Once in Detroit, his work kept him very busy. Time just slipped away. Smiling to myself, I realize we only see each other when he is reassigned to a new parish. Maybe I should make the effort to visit him more often. For today, I'm glad I'm getting this chance to drive him to his new assignment.

It's not only the handsomeness of my brother that would attract any woman's heart. It's also his clothes. Much like a solder's uniform attracts most girls, Tommy's cleric collar does the same. He wears his profession with simple confidence.

I'm often sad thinking about the many joys Tommy and some lucky woman will miss. But now, sitting next to my little brother, I see first hand his shining eyes and joyous heart. He has told me many times that he is married. To The Church. I realize now how wrong my dream would be for him.

As a young boy, my brother always seemed able to read my thoughts. And he did so again the day he became a priest. I must have been showing my sorrow at his ordination, since he told me not to worry about his never being in love. He was in love. With God and His only Son. Our Savior.

Seeing the competent and confident man he's become, despite the horrific parish he's presided over for the last five years, inspires me. He's shown me a way of life far different than I see elsewhere in the world. The abundant love and tolerance it takes to help those less lucky than I. He's continuing to regale me with tales of his days in Detroit. As he talks about troubling lives and tough times, he adds such a touch of love and lightness I can only laugh at his lighthearted humor.

Although my doubling over with laughter while driving may not be a smart thing.

My thoughts are prophetic. Time suddenly seems to slow. Much in that way moviemakers show us events unfolding. Events they want to emphasize. That's how I see the car on the side street running its red light.

It's as though I've stepped outside myself to slowly watch the accident. Since Tommy and I are looking at each other, he never notices the car coming toward him. The car that causes a look of horror to cross my face.

The other car seems to slow as it smashes into Tommy's window. As though it's trying to maneuver its way through a mass of molasses. Its brakes squeal trying to wrench the ton of deadly metal to a halt. The rear end of the car bucks back and forth as the driver desperately tries to stop.

Tommy is still smiling and chatting, although I can see a look of concern begin to appear on his face. His head starts to turn toward where my eyes are affixed in horror. At that moment, the car hits. As my air bag inflates, I regret not insisting on a car with a passenger air bag also. I see my little brother's head bang on the dash as I'm rudely pushed into my seat by a large white air bag.

Silly what one thinks during times of distress. I wonder how a car wreck can attract so many people so quickly. I think it strange that my air bag totally deflates. Those strange little thoughts during a time of trauma. Then I realize airbags only inflate for the instant of impact. Smart engineering I decide.

Now, there's only silence. The screeching tires no longer echo between the city buildings. Suddenly I worry about my brother. If he's hurt. How was I able to so callously forget my own flesh and blood for even a moment? I yank my head toward Tommy and see him slumped forward.

"Tommy. Tommy. Are you okay?" I say. I try to keep the hysteria out of my voice but know I'm failing. As I reach toward my brother's head, I realize the other car has backed away and the crowd is rushing to help.

I find myself thinking inane thoughts. Why do so many people want to help? But isn't it nice, after where Tommy's been for five years? He now gets to see a truly decent side of humanity.

A man is trying to force open my car door. Why doesn't it easily open? I know it worked earlier today.

I shake my head to clear my mind. I have to start thinking clearly. It's obvious there's been an accident. My panic is slowly starting to fade.

I again try to get a response from my brother. Blood is running from a cut above his left eye. A cut covering an area of forehead that is quickly turning blue.

The passenger door finally comes loose with the sound of ripping metal. Two large men pull it open. One bends into the car. "Are you okay?" He asks.

The other man holds the people back. The crowd is being insistent on seeing what happened. "It's just a little accident," he says. "Everyone stay back. We want to make sure the people inside are okay. Please stay back." His firmness increases with each repetition.

"I think I'm fine but I'm worried about my brother," I say.

The crowd outside the car is becoming louder. It's as though I've detached myself from my surroundings. I can hear snatches of conversation taking place among the mass of people surrounding my car.

One woman seems truly upset as she sees Tommy's black shirt and priest's collar. She crosses herself as she exclaims, "He's a priest!" Obviously in distress, she continues, "There is no God."

As if by magic, Tommy's head starts to stir under my hand.

I am profoundly relieved when I realize I haven't just killed my little brother. I pet his head, keeping my hand far from what is becoming an ugly lump above his eye. "Tommy, are you all right?"

He seems to be coming back to us. He asks, "Where am I? What happened?"

"We've had a bit of an accident. I'm afraid you hit the dashboard really hard with your head. We should get you to the hospital. Right now." I've always liked ordering my brother around.

As in the past, my order goes unheard. Tommy looks at me as his eyes continue to clear. "No, I'm okay." His hand goes to the part of his head that is obviously hurt. He gingerly touches a very big bump, then exclaims. "Ohhhh. That does hurt." He hesitates, and then continues, "But honest, I'm okay." He winces as his hand rubs over the injury.

"Tommy," I say, trying to look stern. I feel a terrible guilt rumbling in my belly. "Don't you think it would be smart for us to take you to the hospital? To be sure you're okay?" I want a professional to alleviate my guilt. I want to pass the responsibility to a doctor.

Again Tommy's hand goes to the bump on his forehead as he says, "Really, Maggie. I'm fine." His fingers lightly touch the swelling. "Except for this. And it hurts like Hell." Realizing what he has said, he sheepishly smiles. And adds, "Hell can hurt, you know. So, how's the car?"

Chapter 1

Tommy

I slowly awaken from my deep sleep and am conscious of a recurring fact. A fact I now have frequently. Not a fact, as much as a sensation of movement. A feeling in my soul as I go through that strange transition from deep sleep to awareness. As a kid I often thought this feeling was just my attempt to get back into my body before becoming fully awake. Somehow I thought I might die if I wasn't back inside my body by the time I awoke. It's silly the thoughts I had as a child.

As my eyes open more fully, I look on the wall at the picture of our Savior, Jesus Christ. I've always known in my heart that a life of sacrifice for God and His only Son would be well worth any discomforts being a priest might impose upon me. It's only recently I've had misgivings.

Lying in my bed, I try being objective as I look at the picture. I see a man hanging on a cross. If it weren't for the obvious symbolism, I'm sure the holier-than-thou crowd would be screaming about the violence portrayed in this picture. For God's sake, Jesus has nails through his body parts and a bleeding gash in his side. Despite the gruesomeness depicted, I've had years of comfort viewing this very picture each morning.

I received the picture on my tenth birthday. My memory takes me to that morning so many years ago. I was so excited when I awoke and remembered what day it was. I ran down the stairs from my bedroom, knowing I was going to be given something unique. It was the O'Malley way, making the tenth birthday special. I remembered my brother and sister's excitement on each of their own birthdays years earlier when they had turned ten. Finally it was my day. A memorable day. As I entered the kitchen, my mom turned to me and said, "Happy birthday, Tommy. My, you look much more mature. And taller." I knew she was teasing me in her loving way. With a big smile on her face, she asked, "What can I make for your breakfast?"

I remember having dreamed all night long about my birthday breakfast. And how I could make it uniquely mine. I'd hardly been able to close my eyes. After a long and deliberate analysis, I had decided that I'd have three eggs, not my normal two. And ham instead of bacon. And, of course, as much toast and jam as I could eat. I gave Mom my order. She smiled and turned to the stove to prepare my request. I was unable to withhold my excitement another minute. My voice cracking with excitement as I asked my mother, "When do I get to open my presents?" I knew I'd be getting a special present from my mother and father. I'd also get something from my older brother and sister.

"Not until you eat all of your breakfast and then we go to Mass," she answered. She knew I loved going to our church and listening to the strange language the priest spoke. "Given the size of the breakfast you requested, I'd say you'd better eat quickly so we're not late for Mass." She set in front of me a huge platter filled with all the food I'd ordered. I was so excited. I was no longer a little kid.

I remember fondly opening all my presents those many years ago. As I had expected, my brother and sister had given me toys. But toys befitting someone of my advanced age, I had thought then. Now, years later, I can't even remember what they had given me. I do remember, though, the pride I felt from their thinking me mature. But more than anything, I will never forget the present I received from my parents that year. The very picture I'm looking at now. A print of the famous Daphne mosaic depicting The Crucifixion.

Deciding I'd better get moving and stop my foolish nostalgia, I swing my legs from the bed, and put on my old hand-me-down slippers. I have kept them because a favorite parishioner in Detroit had given them to me. He had insisted they still had years of use left in them. As the fog continues to clear from my mind, the reason I set my alarm comes back to me. I'd promised my friend Jim I'd go jogging with him. For some un-Godly reason, he thinks it's healthy to jog as the sun comes up. When I have occasionally allowed his good nature to overcome my good sense and actually go jogging with him, I wonder why anyone would willingly do this to themselves.

In my overly large slippers, I shuffle along down the hallway to the bathroom. I'm sure if I'd buy some slippers that fit, I'd be able to walk normally. I look at the large grandfather clock sitting in the rectory. Its only fifteen minutes before Jim will come jogging to the door, so I rush through my early morning ablutions.

A little jogging to warm me up won't hurt, I suppose. I'm trying to get a better outlook on this exercising thing. Maybe I should bless Jim for forcing me to do this. But then, remembering how torturous jogging can be, I doubt I'll even thank him. Certainly not bless him.

I met Jim at college. He'd been the one fellow in his fraternity who had thought my shyness wouldn't be a liability to his social life. At the time I couldn't imagine why. He had quite a reputation for being wild and a womanizer. I'd heard about him and his friends. And the hard rock band they'd put together in his garage. I'd also heard about the wild adventures the band members had each summer while on the road playing music in every honky-tonk in the state. I couldn't understand why he would befriend someone like me. A book freak that had more interest in Socrates than sex.

After arriving on the campus at the age of eighteen, I'd been lonely for family and friendship. So I decided to see what was meant by "rush week" in the fraternity community. I'd wanted to continue living at home and attend a nearby school, but my parents thought differently. They assured me the apron strings should be broken. They sent me to the state college more than a hundred miles from home. I now understand their motivation. But as a young man, I was traumatized.

The first two weeks away from home were glum. Since I hadn't chosen a roommate before arriving on campus, one had been selected for me. Todd. After getting to know Todd, I understood why he didn't have anyone to room with.

I had no preconceived ideas about a person being over-weight, although as a child I had been blessed with abundant energy that kept me skinny. Todd apparently wasn't so blessed. His hugeness wasn't the problem. Even his insistence on passing gas as a form of humor wouldn't have stopped any friendship. His constant flatulence wasn't too bad by itself. It was his horselaugh. When the smell from his most recent intestinal eruption swept the room, he would roll on the floor in howls of hysteria. His horselaugh echoing off the walls.

That was the last straw. On my second Friday night, being so far from home, I knew I had to become responsible for my own life. I knew I had to find a better living situation. Why not a fraternity?

The first fraternity I entered was Delta Chi. Jim was just inside the door greeting the freshmen. As we got to talking, I could feel our friendship begin.

Now, years later, as I prepare to intercept him as he jogs past the church, I know the truth about Jim. His womanizing reputation was not valid. If he did go wild for a couple summers, it was only experimental, not a life long thing. His academic and philosophic nature took him to law school and then into a successful practice. If it weren't for this crazy jogging obsession, I'd think the man was perfect.

Chapter 2

I quickly finish brushing my teeth, thinking about the many moronic rituals of man. I've realized for years that I'm in the ritual business. It's what I sell. Some men sell cars, or clothes, or even food. I sell rituals. And I've taken comfort in the job for all this time. It's not that I've become cynical about the ritual thing or the sales aspect. On a daily basis, I see the happiness hope can bring. On the other hand, how can I continue selling a ritual proclaiming a God I myself have learned to doubt?

My love affair with the ritualistic life began early. When I was a kid, my parents would pack the whole family into the car and take us to Mass. Usually three times a week. Whereas my older brother and sister thought this a travesty to their freedom, I found it comforting. In church, I knew what to expect and I felt close to God. It's as though God was talking to me alone, as the priest would mumble the same words week after week at every service.

Unlike my brother and sister who had squirmed in the uncomfortable pews, I sat with my eyes closed and tried to mimic the priest's words. I knew that if I could say those words as accurately as the white robed priest was saying them, I too would be loved by God. Not knowing Latin, I had not a clue what the words meant. I only knew they were the words preferred by God. And I knew I must learn how to communicate with God.

Opening the door to leave the small bathroom, I see my Monsignor. Monsignor Ramón let me know, when I first arrived at his parish, that he didn't stand on ceremony. He told me he thought the title "Monsignor" was a bit presumptuous, insisting I call him Ramón whenever we're alone. Granting his wish, I now think of this short fat man as Ramón, not to lessen his character but as a sign of deep respect. I couldn't wish for a dearer friend and mentor.

Smiling as he carefully comes down the steps from his second floor bedroom, he looks up and says, "Hi, Tommy. I see your friend has again talked you into an early morning run. Good for him." He must see the scowl on my face. His own face brightens even more. "It will do you good, my boy. God loves the industrious."

"Why don't you join us this morning?" I counter. I'm only trying to get his goat. Ramón is from Spain. In that country, afternoon naps are more important than exercise. But I never tire of our verbal sparring. Ramón's a joy to be near.

I've loved and profited by my months working under him. Whereas I'm tall and thin, he is as round as a bowling ball and not much taller. I've tried rattling the man. Thus far, I've failed. I continue, "A little running might help you lose some of that extra weight I've been noticing." I indicate his protruding waistline.

His smile becomes a chuckle. He responds, "No, my dear man. I shan't be doing any exercising. I won't be tarnishing that which I've worked so hard to gain." He pats his belly that's poking from his robe. Then continues, "Now, if you'll just get out of the way, I can finish my morning paper in here." He nudges me aside and enters the bathroom I've just vacated. As the door closes, I hear his voice booming through the wall. "Be sure to say hi to Jim for me. And have a successful run," he chuckles.

As I shuffled back to my bedroom, I thought about how I had come to work under Ramón. Right after being ordained, I was blessed by an assignment in "God's Country," the mountains of Colorado. Following those two blessed years, I was assigned to a diocese in the poorest part of downtown Detroit. Compared to Detroit, this diocese with Ramón is a walk in the park. In my neighborhood in Detroit, even the churches had to have locks on the doors and bars over the windows. I learned first hand about the damage caused by drugs. Drugs that can ravish the spirit and cause drug dependence. A dependence that even the fear of God can't overcome.

Our church's collection box was to the left of the main entrance. We left the collection box near the front door with the hope that those coming for comfort during off hours would leave a little something to help the neighborhood. The collection box was strong steel and heavily locked. Even with that protection, we'd often find it had been broken into when we'd collect the meager money that had been left. Thievery is the legacy of poverty and drugs.

After five long years in Detroit, I was told Ramón had requested I join him in this peaceful place. Despite his outward appearance of well being, I knew Ramón was ill and had only a short time left. His parish and in fact the whole community will miss him.

In learning about his history, I found out that, before coming here, Ramon had also spent many years working with the poor. One doesn't become a Monsignor by ministering to the middle class.

I enter my adequate bedroom to don my almost brand new jogging outfit. Looking again at my watch, I realize that Jim's going to be coming past the front of the rectory any minute now. I toss my robe onto my unmade bed and retrieve my jogging shorts.

My outrageously colored shorts were a gift from Jim when he first talked me into taking these morning runs with him. True to his mischievous spirit, the shorts are bright chartreuse, with comic characters jogging circles around my body. I pull on the shorts and sit on the side of the bed to lace my shoes.

Jim and I went our own way after graduating from college, he to law school and me to the seminary. Despite that, we've managed to keep in touch. Jim planned to help mankind by becoming an attorney. My plan involved God. When we did get together, he would laugh at my seriousness and say there was more than one way to bring hope to man. I was never sure if Jim had the proper respect for God or God's only Son, our Savior. I worry now that I might have lost that respect myself.

I finish tying my shoes and head toward the front of the church. As I step out of the door and onto the street, I see Jim jogging toward me. My timing is impeccable. In the past, this coincidence would have proven to me the existence of God. Always before, I would have attributed my perfect timing as a

Godly miracle. I've felt it was God's Divine Hand on my shoulder that produced this type of miracle in my life. My faith is more conventional now. I see a coincidence for what it is.

Jim notices me and gives a wave. I excuse the outrageous color of the jogging shorts he had given me with the thought that he must have bad eyesight. He must feel the bright color is the only way he will be able to find me if I ever get lost in a crowd. Jogging toward me, he looks down at my chartreuse shorts and grins. I wave away any idea of bad eyes. He's just a devil in disguise, having his devilish fun.

I step in beside him and begin to jog as he smoothly continues his pace. "How are you this morning?" I ask.

He looks at me and smiles. "You look grumpy." His face takes on an insincere seriousness. I know that look. "Tommy," he continues, "I think I've discovered your problem. There just aren't enough souls to save in this town. What with our wealth and our Starbuck's, we just naturally shine in the eyes of God. If I didn't so much enjoy running with you, and picking on you, I'd suggest you go back to your slums where you were most happy."

We continue our ongoing banter as I get into the running rhythm. I feel my muscles starting to stretch. It's becoming easier to keep up Jim's speed. I never have a problem keeping up with his banter when we're sitting down. As I think about it, that's probably why he takes me jogging. He thinks the lack of oxygen in my brain will give him an edge in our verbal wars.

I tell him this and he chuckles. Then, as if to confirm my fear, he increases his speed, causing me to fall back. Struggling to catch up, I continue our good-humored jesting. "I think, my dear Jimmy, God actually most loves those who are destitute. Always remember, 'the humble shall inherit the Earth.' I see a lacking of humbleness in this suburb." I wave my arm in a wide arc, taking in the entire city I see.

I've paraphrased the Good Book. I rationalize by saying my statement is voiced only to get a rise out of Jim. More verbal sparing. Although, as the words leave my lips, I realize I once believed this sentiment. Until recently, I believed that those mired in materialism had a tougher time making it to Heaven. Now I wonder if I haven't actually wasted the last ten years of my own life. A more materialistic life might not be so bad after all.

My head jerks left as I hear screeching brakes. Someone hoping to get his car stopped before it bashes into another. I barely avoid stumbling. I pull my thoughts back to Jim and the sentiment I just stated. If God loves the humble, why do men like Jim, with their fantastic self-assurance, live so well? And do so well? A black thought seeps deep into my soul. A thought I've been steeling myself against. There just couldn't be a God. Otherwise, people wouldn't be so rewarded for having abundant wealth. The meek just seem to fall further and further behind.

I notice, just like the rest of the meek humans, I'm falling further behind Jim. I ratchet up my pace to catch up with him.

Chapter 3

As I again pull up beside Jim, I notice he's apparently reached that place serious athletes call "the zone." They always seem to say this term with a mysterious little tilt to their heads. As though they alone know a secret. I don't have personal experience with this particular phenomenon but have heard Jim and other athletes talk about it often. So often do joggers and even professional athletes mention it, I have no doubt it exists.

Jim's face looks peaceful. It's not that he isn't here. It's more as though he is very much here but not letting the earthly tethers of his body bother him. When I hear athletes describing the zone, I wonder how they can ever doubt the existence of a soul. It makes sense to me that once a person realizes he's escaped the restrictions of his body, he must then recognize that he is more a spirit. Not a body. The only logical conclusion is that he is a soul.

Suddenly, a jolting possibility occurs to me. Maybe I've found the source of my recent lack of faith. Could it be because I've never experienced this other-worldliness? Perhaps a person in the zone is no longer chained to this world. Perhaps they have risen to a higher state, where they don't inhabit the body, but only control it. Much as a racecar driver gets into and out of cars. A racecar driver never becomes confused, thinking he is a car. He knows he is only controlling his car. I wonder if I might rise to this higher state of being ness if I try running faster. Might I also realize that I'm only controlling my body? I am me, not my body.

These philosophic flights of fancy are distracting me from my jogging. Again I'm trailing Jim. I see him, a half block ahead, turning the last corner that will lead us to the lake in the park.

More times than not, we run around the lake to get our five miles in. I can't complain about the route since it's much preferable to dodging cars and trucks on the street.

If I have any hope of finding that place called the zone, I'm going to have to speed up and run at Jim's pace. I push my muscles harder and again pull up beside him. I pray that once I've discovered the zone for myself, I'll never again doubt the existence of God.

We cross the street and start to follow the recreation path circling the lake. I notice other joggers, also seeming to enjoy this un-godly sport. Possibly, they too have released themselves from bodily tethers, and aren't feeling the pain I'm experiencing.

As close as I ever came to reaching the zone was in a sixth grade gym class. I had been asked by the fastest runners in my grade to join their relay team. Although I beamed with pride at being chosen by the best of our class, I couldn't imagine why they had chosen me. I had the reputation of being the teacher's pet, not a fast runner. Possibly they thought I'd help them with homework or give them special privileges when I was class monitor.

Whatever they were thinking, I found myself on their team, the third runner in a squad of four. The fastest runner was the last runner. I think they put me as the third runner to give me the best chance of helping to win.

I remember watching the first runners take off. Our team was in first place when my teammate handed the baton to our next runner. He also took off like a shot. As he rounded the far corner, coming near to my handoff, I realized he had me so far in front I couldn't possible mess up. My heart pumped, as he got nearer. My time in the sun was rapidly approaching.

He accurately placed the baton in my hand. He didn't even allow me to make a mistake. I felt him take his other hand and gently but firmly close my fingers around the baton. With friends like this, I'd never be a loser. I took off. Actually, at that moment, I might have found the zone. I could see my small body shoot away from my starting point. What I had thought were scrawny legs suddenly seemed to become sinewy. Although I was not nearly as fast as my teammates, I didn't seem to be losing any time to the other runners. I was holding my own.

Suddenly I realized I was seeing my body from a distance and I panicked. I knew I wasn't supposed to be looking at my body running. In some way, even at my young age, I'd been taught I was supposed to be inside my body. That moment of doubt is all it took. After having gotten so rapidly into the zone, I just as quickly came out of that mysterious place. I was again firmly planted inside my body. Again seeing where I was going, the dirt moving swiftly beneath my feet. My lungs begging for a breath, screaming for relieve.

I looked to see how far I still had to run before I reached the last runner in our team. His arm was stretched backwards, getting ready for the handoff. I worried I couldn't make it. And with that loss of faith, I tripped and fell to my face. I'd been running so fast that I actually skidded on my nose across the track.

All the other runners ran past me as I lay on the ground trying to get back up. My teammates ran to my aid. Although they were helpful in getting me to my feet and wiping away the blood, I could tell they were disappointed with my performance. From that point on, I always felt the idea of being in the zone was just a fantasy, or at best a hurtful place.

From the perspective of a mature man, I wonder if I hadn't confused the cause of my accident. Maybe it was the doubt that caused me to fall. Being in the zone might actually have been a benefit. If only I hadn't doubted it's existence.

If I could just overcome that childish embarrassment, maybe I could run as effortlessly as Jim. I renew my determination to run beside Jim. I figure if I match his easy gait, then I'll also know the joy of being in the zone. But, my spirit is broken with Jim's next words.

"I think I'll pick up the pace a bit. I'll wait up for you on the other side of the lake." He indicates a covered bench where we often take a break. He moves away from me as though I'm standing still.

Chapter 4

It's been clear to me from an early age that I'm not a jock. I knew, even before the embarrassing relay incident in the sixth grade, that I had little athletic ability. Seeing how quickly Jim is pulling away from my slow jog only reinforces this conclusion. I settle into a comfortable speed, and try to take an interest in the trees and other foliage around me.

Suddenly from behind, I hear my name. "Father O'Malley. Is that you?" A pleasant female voice.

I slow even more and look back to see Sandra. As she pulls up next to me, she asks, "Are you jogging alone?"

My heart actually beats quicker upon seeing Sandra Johnson. She's a very attractive young lady who started coming to my Sunday Mass soon after I arrived in this city. I've tried to look at her as only another soul to save, but the images of her easy smile and attractive features invade my thinking many times a day. Not another soul, but a beautiful woman. Possibly this quiet community has darkened my character. I've never before had problems with temptations of the flesh, no matter what wonderful beauty would sit in my pews.

I smile saying, "No. I'm afraid my friend Jim gets tired of going slow with me. We'll be meeting over there." I indicate the other side of the lake where the resting area is.

"Do you mind if I join you?" she asks. "I get really bored with my own thoughts when I jog."

"I'd love the company. Do you jog here often?" I notice that her jogging shoes and shorts are far more worn than mine. She looks more accomplished at this sport than I. I worry that I might again embarrass myself with my athletic ineptitude. Although, if I embarrass myself now, it'll not be in front of a bunch of sixth grade boys but in front of a beautiful young woman.

"No," she answers. "Actually, I prefer running to the north and into the hills. I love seeing the deer and sometimes even other animals around there. Although recently I've been using this path more often "

As I continue the pleasant chatter with Sandra, I recognize my thoughts are becoming inappropriate for someone in my profession. I realize how enjoyable an attractive female companion can be. It's not as though I've never noticed the differences and advantages offered by the fairer sex. As an adolescent, I seemed to attract a number of pretty girls as admirers and had even enjoyed their company. What had amazed me was that they seemed to enjoy my company as well.

Men are often afraid that women are only attracted to the bad boys or the macho athletic type. My experience has been different. It seemed that my love of philosophy and my examination of the condition of mankind was attractive to the cheerleader set. I've often wondered why. I decide to put this question to Sandra.

"You're an attractive woman, and single," I say. I notice her eyes widen in some surprise, so I hasten to add, "As they say in the vernacular, I'm not hitting on you. But I am curious about how women feel." I hesitate, not being sure if I should actually continue. Then I ask, "Will I embarrass you if I continue this conversation?"

Whatever shock I had caused Sandra by my first comment on the subject quickly turned to a bemused and slightly mischievous smile. "No. Of course not. And even if you are hitting on me, I'd be flattered," she says, smiling even more girlishly. "But then, we can't forget, you are forbidden territory."

Now it's my turn to be embarrassed. I feel my face turn red with heat. My embarrassment only increases Sandra's enjoyment. "Oh, don't worry Father. I won't attack you. What is it you want to ask? Any topic is fair game." Her eyes seem to be sparkling.

She had given me the opening I had hoped for. I rationalize that my interest is only research into an area about which I have little knowledge, I boldly continue. "Uhhh. Well, . . . " I stammer.

"Actually, what's going on right now is what I want to ask about. When I was a teenager, . . ." I'm still faltering in my question. "And then continuing when I was in college, . . ."

I notice that Sandra's eyes are taking on that confused look I sometimes notice when I'm making no sense and my audience has no clue what I'm talking about. I try to keep my mind on the question I want Sandra to answer. But I'm concerned what Sandra might think of my un-priestly thoughts. I worry that what I'm calling research, she might think is lechery. I really have no idea what women consider bawdy behavior. On the other hand, if, as I've recently come to fear, there is no God, why am I denying myself the pleasures of a lifelong companion such as Sandra? Or the heavenly joys of the physical union, which accompanies such a relationship.

Sandra continues to patiently look over at me as we continue our jogging. With her pleasant smile, she is encouraging me to speak. There's no denying that she would make as lovely a life companion as she makes a jogging companion. I take the bull by the horns.

"Well. I've had this problem with females. Even as a teenager." I look at her to see how she might be taking this and realize she's gotten entirely the wrong idea. Her look and slight nod of her head indicates she thinks I'm going to confess a homosexual type secret. Until now, I always thought it humorous how people view priests. The first explanation many people have for a priest's electing celibacy involves either impotence or homosexuality. Since neither of those conditions is a problem I experience, I'm shocked at Sandra's sudden look. I hurry to clear up the possible misconception.   "From a very young age, I've been intrigued by the rituals of The Church and the love of God."

Sandra began to frown. I learned early in my career that I had to watch what effect my words were having on my audience while delivering my weekly sermon. That lesson applied even when the audience was just one person. A speaker had better be alert to the listener's reaction to his utterances. My words have confused Sandra, but at least I've disabused her of thinking of me as a homosexual. Now, I'd like to see if she could consider me an attractive man.

"I never hid my interest in spiritual matters, even though I knew my friends were interested in girls." As a postscript, I add, "I was truly happy for each of my friends, as they'd weave their way through that adolescent maze of uncertainty to find love." I smiled, recalling the banter my friends and I had on this subject. "They would say I was jealous of their exciting sexual adventures. But, in fact, I had already found love with God. I was glad for them when they also found love. Even if it was of a less heavenly sort."

By Sandra's response, I realize my communication on this topic with Sandra isn't going well. She slows down to a walk, then heads toward a tree and stands in its shade. I also slow down and then come to a halt in front of her. Looking at her, I see how perplexed she has become. She looks up at me and asks, "Are you saying you fell in love with God? Not in some, uhhhh.... vague religious sort of way. But, in the same way the rest of us think of love?" She waves her hand in the air to indicate some ambiguous concept. She's obviously not as confused as her eyes seem to indicate. But she is discomforted.

Why is it so impossible for a layperson to understand that we priests fall in love also? In fact, usually that's why we became priests. Most women, and even many men, would agree that true love comes from the heart and not the flesh. Why then is it so difficult to believe I fell in love with God, even though he has no flesh to tempt me?

I'm nodding to indicate that she has the essence of what I've said. I continue, "But therein lies a curious problem which I've had for many years. As soon as a woman realizes I love God, I become a challenge." Realizing what I've said might be construed as an accusation against Sandra, I hasten to say. "Not all women. But it has happened. And I wonder why? A woman who would never consider breaking up a marriage or tempting another woman's man seems to think I'm fair game."

Sandra hangs her head. I fear I've made a very bad mistake. During my many years as a priest, I've noticed a recurring phenomenon. Parents probably recognize this same pattern with their children. If I inadvertently get close to a person's private secrets, but don't actually get the secret stated, that person will become very guilt ridden. And sometimes even hostile. I've often considered this behavior to be the source of adolescent rebellion. It is certainly the foundation of one of The Church's basic beliefs.

Having opened this can of worms with Sandra, I now need to put her to rights. Laying my hand on her shoulders, and then raising her head so she looks at me, I say, "Actually, I have a confession."

She looks shocked, then says, "I thought that was my line."

We both smile. Then, we both start to speak at the same time, but she continues. "I can see why you've had that problem with women. To a woman, there's nothing quite as sweet as the forbidden fruit."

I have to give her credit. Whereas earlier, she hung her head in shame, she now stands defiantly before me and is locking my eyes with hers. "It's true that we women often want the bad boy. But that's only so we can rehabilitate him. Think how much more we've proven our feminine worth if we can win the heart of a man who has forsaken all women for God"

I've obviously created a problem. I have to explain my newly changed attitude about God before this adorable creature becomes so guilt-ridden I will never again see her outside of my church. I start to speak.

She puts her hand on my mouth to prevent my interrupting. "I am so sorry Father. As you explained earlier, I never thought about the possibility that you might simply be in love with God. It's an abstraction that I'm ashamed to say I never considered. I would never steal another person's mate. But I actually have looked at you in a romantic way. And I had thoughts of stealing your heart. In fact, I started coming to your church because of you."

I have to give her credit. Her eyes never waver from mine as she states her confession. I'm startled by what she has just said and my heart begins beating faster. As I continue to stand very near to Sandra, with my heart beating madly, I realize that my rushing blood is not because of the exercise. Sandra's body almost touching mine, causing a burning emotion that leaves me lightheaded.

I remember first noticing Sandra while delivering Mass my

second Sunday in this new parish. She was sitting in the front pew, seemingly by herself. I continued to notice her in the same seat each of the following Sundays and began to look forward to seeing her. Her youthful demeanor was intoxicating.

Until I moved from Detroit, I'd never had any doubt of my love of God. Nor any temptation toward seeking the physical pleasures of a woman. But, since arriving in this diocese, it's become easier and easier to contemplate loving a woman like Sandra. I'm saddened by this withering away of my love for God and my doubting His existence. Although this sadness at times has been replaced by daydreams of Sandra. Or women like Sandra. But as I stand so near her with our hands on each other's arms, my heart leaps as I realize my fanciful feelings toward her have somehow been reciprocal. For the first time in my life, my lips touch a woman's, in a light caress. I want to explain to her feelings I have trouble understanding myself.

Before I get an opportunity to speak, Sandra says, "We'd better get going or your friend will be wondering what wicked woman waylaid his priestly friend." She's smiling broadly as she says this.

Whatever guilt she felt seems to have vanished. Or at least she's not going to allow it to hurt our friendship. For this, I am thankful. I realize that this is a woman I'd truly love to get to know better. But first I need to tell her what is lying so heavily in my heart.

Chapter 5

As Sandra takes off jogging, her tightly clad body swaying attractively for my eyes, I remember my first love. My first female love. It was, after all, after I had given my heart to our Lord and His Church.

That first female object of my love sang in the choir during Sunday morning services. Her hair had a brilliant radiance as if she wore a halo, and her eyes had a glow I believed came from her love of our Lord. I would sit in my pew admiring her from afar. My best friend was dating her best friend. That was how I found out the important things about her. At fourteen, she was a year younger than me, and her name was Sally. I fantasized that by the time we would wed, The Church would have changed its prohibition on priest's marrying. Within six months, Sally's father was transferred to Oregon. I was never again to see her. My dream was gone.

I never again saw Sally. I never did hear her voice in conversation, only in song. I vowed not to make the same mistake by failing to tell Sandra how I felt. Hurrying to catch up again to a quickly disappearing Sandra, I realize why Sally came to my mind. Same color hair. Same slim body. Same sweet face. Sandra is the woman I imagined Sally would have become.

I catch up and keep stride with Sandra, tying not to notice how much she's slowed her pace. She apparently realizes it's the only way I'll be able to run beside her. I look at her as she keeps up a steady stream of conversation about the beauty of the park and the lake and lawn we get to enjoy. Again I decide I must tell her about my feelings for her.

How should I start?

Feigning a chuckle, I say, "When I was a mere lad, I fell head over heels for a girl in the choir." I watch her face intently to see how my words affect her. Her face doesn't show a twitch; as though she knows her silence will encourage me to continue. "Except for hearing her sing, I never once heard her voice," I say.

This admission seems to have perked her interest. "Is that when you decided to become a priest?" she asks. The look in her eyes shows sincere sympathy. I see that I've again put forth the wrong message.

"Oh, no," I exclaim. "I was already in love with God. I started loving God when I was about eight or nine." I realize I now have the perfect opportunity to say what I want to say. "My love for God never diminished." Adding sadly, "That is, until recently."

She again gives me a sympathetic look. Although this time, I also see a large amount of concern. She takes the conversation in a direction I'm not sure I want to broach. She says, "What caused your love to diminish, Father?" I'm sure she meant no harm with her question, although I feel I've been demoted. She is again referring to me as Father O'Malley, the priest and not Tommy, the man.

I've often heard criticism that priests are allowed to give marital advice. "How," the argument goes, "can a man that's never been married have the slightest idea what married men are going through? Much less, how women think?" In my case, the criticism is accurate. I don't even know the preliminaries of courting a female, much less marrying one. Never having dated a girl, I now find I haven't a clue how to keep this topic of conversation going in the direction I had planned.

My friend Jim would often tease me about women, saying that I don't know what I'm missing. I've never had to guess what a woman might be thinking. He'd say, when it came to topics of the heart, women will insist that you read their minds accurately or they become insufferable. I wondered why Sandra was now thinking of me as a priest. What could be in her mind? Jim was right, loving the Church, and God, is much easier.

I'm unsure of how to respond to Sandra's question. I stammer, trying to think of a way to tell Sandra how much she reminds me of that long ago girl in the choir. The love that I had lost.

Concerning Sandra's last question, I decide to use a technique I learned while giving advice to newly married couples. They would talk openly about their sexual lives, as though I knew about everything they mentioned. Actually, they might as well have been speaking Greek for all I understood. So I learned to pay no heed to those topics I knew nothing about and ignored their comments. I now did likewise with Sandra.

I ignore Sandra's comment and again try to get her to understand my feelings toward her. "The girl's name was Sally. You remind me so much of her."

A look of absolute confusion shoots across Sandra's face, and then is quickly replaced by fear.

When I fell in love with God at the tender age of eight, I must have been prophetic. Even though I was much too young to have those hormonal stirrings I'd later learn were love or lust, I knew one fact for sure. If I loved God, that love would never present to me the type of difficulties a man has when courting a woman of the flesh. I don't want Sandra to have any confusion. I certainly don't want her to have fear. "I didn't mean to upset you," I say as I slow to a walk. She slows also, then walks with me to lean against a near by shade tree.

I don't normally find so many excuses to take breaks in my morning jog, but this morning, the anxiety I feel from talking to this beautiful woman about love and lust is causing me confusion and guilt. If I weren't already overwrought with such conflicting shame, I'd undoubtedly also feel guilty about the number of excuses I'm finding to not jog.

"Sandra," I say as I try to catch my breath. I had suspected she'd been running slowly for my benefit and now it's obvious. She's breathing easily and normally. "Sandra," I gasp again. "Since the first time you came into my church, I've been taken by you. I've enjoyed watching your young beauty and your vitality." I notice a continuing mix of confusion, fear, and now embarrassment flowing in equal parts across her face.

Her hand comes up to my arm as I try continuing my explanation. Her touch is a jolt to my senses. Is it possible that I've lived thirty-five years and never had a woman, other than a relative, touch me? Possibly a handshake, but nothing as personal as Sandra is now doing. I've certainly never been in the situation I now find myself. Emotions are ravaging my mind.

"Father, I find myself in a strange position," Sandra says. She laughs a strangely cynical half-laugh. "I guess I could say a thing I've often said in the privacy of a small booth. Father, forgive me for I have sinned."

She takes her hand from my arm. I realize what she has done. With those words, her viewpoint of me has changed. I am now her Father Confessor and no longer an attractive man. In the past, I would have always considered a priest more lofty in the hierarchy of man. In my current condition, though, I feel my rank has been reduced. I've been downgraded from an appealing man to a member of the priesthood. The loss of status depresses me.

Again, I'm taken by her spunk. She looks me in the eye as she continues, "I have to confess, Father. It's like you said earlier. I was playing a little game with your feelings and now I feel so ashamed." Her eyes drop to the ground, but then again with a determined jut of her jaw, she looks up at me. "You are a very attractive man. But even more than that. You're forbidden." I can tell from the slight relaxing of her muscles that she has finally said it. It is a wondrous thing to see the miracle brought about from purging oneself of guilt.

Her eyes stay locked onto mine. But now they take on a glow of propriety. I'm afraid the time for guilt and confession is soon going to be mine.

"Father, I ask you again. Please tell me. It's important. What recently caused you to stop loving God?"

Before I was ordained, I made it a habit to go to confession at least once a week. I began that practice at my First Communion when I was eight. Since becoming a priest, I've continued my weekly confessions. Though now less ritual is involved. The Church has decided that we priests can confess directly to God. I miss the human factor when I relieve myself of my sins in such a way. To add the human touch, I occasionally confess to whichever priest is nearby. Although, in these instances, my confessions are disguised as part of a conversation. I've backslid over the years and have given an earful to many a monsignor.

I've often wondered about the stammering, justifying, rationalizing, and apologizing for sexual misdeeds that I've heard in the confessions of others. Since sins of the flesh haven't before been my area of weakness, I've never had to speak of such matters to a priest. I now find myself in the silly yet serious situation of having to say such things to this young lady.

Chapter 6

"I'm not sure," I temporize. "I've been thinking more and more recently that maybe I've made a terrible mistake with my life." I try looking Sandra in the eye with the same bravado she did me. "I can't say it's entirely because you came into my Church. But the coincidence in time is suspect."

"What do you mean?" She's actually drawing me out. She's showing genuine interest in helping me find the answer to the problem that's been nagging me these last few months.

It would be disingenuous if I didn't at least try to explain what I've come to think of as unexplainable. "I've always described my faith in God as my having a long term love of God. I tried explaining it to you in that way a bit ago. Whenever I've heard men talk about being in love with a woman, they've described the same feeling I've had for God since I was young. It's the same feeling I've recently started to feel for..." I'm having difficulty going ahead with my explanation. I hesitate telling her. I've come to value her. My heart is now in her hands. Looking at Sandra, she nods her head. I realize she understands my meaning without my saying the words.

I've always believed that a sin not confessed is a sin not confronted. So I utter the words. I continue with renewed faith now that I'm thinking of Sandra as my confessor. "I felt the stirring of unfamiliar feelings for that young girl in the choir many years ago. And also... Those same feelings for you within the last few months." There, I said it. I've bared my soul. Why don't I feel the relief that confession is suppose to bring?

Sandra continues to nod her head in an accepting way.

"Father, in most things I have no doubt you are far more wise than I am." She smiles sadly as she continues, "But when it comes to falling in love." She again gives that mischievous elfish smile. "Or that other thing, falling in lust. In either case, I'm sure I have a lot more experience than you do. Do you mind if I give you my opinion, even though I might really be way off base?"

She asks this in such a sincere way, I have no hope of saying no. I nod for her to continue. She starts slowly, and then heats up as she gets into her theory. "When you told me how you felt, being in love with God, it sounded similar to a feeling I've had in my life. That feeling was how I felt for the one man who stole my heart."

I can see she's getting ready to tell me a story of her heartbreak. But, she then shakes the memory away and goes back to telling me her theory about my situation. "In my case, something happened to make me lose my love. And also, in my case, it didn't take much. All he had to do was just be what men often are. A pig!" The last word is spoken with force, with an emotion that is far from Christian. Then, as if by magic, her face again takes on the soft lines of a beautiful woman, as she smiles at herself.

I conclude that the man must have broken her heart by some sort of betrayal. Is she suggesting that God in some way betrayed me? And that I'm paying him back by denying His existence? It's a ponderous thought.

Sandra continues, dragging my attention back to her, "It's why I wonder. And why I asked you. What happened to make you fall out of love with God?"

We both realize we've been doing far more standing than jogging. As a compromise, in order to allow our conversation to continue, we start walking along the jogging path as we talk. She looks at me expectantly as we slowly walk along. I realize she's not going to let me ignore her question. Perhaps I should give her a little history. Possibly only as a stalling device. But it seems appropriate for me to tell her about my happiness in Detroit.

Chapter 7

"After being ordained almost nine years ago, I spent what amounted to an apprenticeship in a small mountain town out west. I wondered why The Church sent me to such an awe-inspiring location. Later, I decided they had sent me there because they already knew about the poverty waiting for me at my next assignment. They apparently first wanted me to know that a paradise on Earth can actually exist." I smile as I remember the small Colorado community.

"The difference between a Catholic diocese in a mountain town and one in a poor area of Detroit is startling. In the Rockies, my main concern was the trouble bored youth would get into. Even the sin of boredom was only an occasional lapse. In a ski community that was also blessed with beautiful summer days, there was no lack of activities. It was easy to keep idle hands from becoming mischievous."

My face takes on a look of peace. "It's as though God had allowed a select few souls to have the abundance of His natural beauties. The people of the community repaid Him by living relatively wholesome lives. That isn't to say drugs didn't cause some chaos in our little hamlet. And also, there was the ever-present temptation of the flesh. Occasionally a young couple would find themselves being parents sooner than they expected. All told, though, God's beauty won the day."

I shake away the idyllic thoughts of the mountains as I continue telling my tale. "After two years of such serenity, I was transferred to a diocese in downtown Detroit. I was struck by the contrast when I drove up to the cathedral in a very poor Detroit neighborhood. In my Colorado community, the church was a relatively new building, built out of rocks quarried from nearby mine tailings. An attractive enough building, but not inspired, unlike the large church in Detroit."

Sandra continues to walk along, occasionally looking down at her feet. Mostly looking at me as I talk. Often nodding encouragement and understanding.

"My sister drove me to my new assignment in the slums. We arrived at a great cathedral, it's spire twirling into the sky, overlooking trashed streets, rusting cars, and boarded up storefronts. I remember shifting my eyes from the beautiful church in front of me to the street which was laying at its feet in such decay."

Sandra's eyes take on a look of sadness to equal my own feelings. I imagine that she's also feeling the sadness for what man must sometimes endure. I continue my story so she's not left with the mistaken belief that I was unhappy in that godforsaken place. "I was soon to learn the truth. The grand church had been built in the heyday of Detroit's auto making history. Those streets had once housed well off factory workers. Most of the community had originally come from Ireland, having found their way to the high paying auto factories. They thought they were living in luxury and built the great church as a way to thank God for His kindness."

I smile slightly as I continue, "It might have been a wry sense of humor of The Church's superiors that sent me, an Irishman, to a community which had been built by people from my own ancestral land. But, by the time I arrived, the Irish were gone. The builders had departed. They were all following the automobile factories to other towns and other states. They left behind them their towering church. They also left behind them the soul scorching poverty."

Sandra doesn't utter a word. She gives me all her attention as I relate to her the impact that assignment had on me. "It was on that day, arriving in the Detroit slums, when I thought I'd finally found my place in God's plan."

My eyes fix on Sandra's eyes. "As I looked back toward the towering church and rectory where I would spend the next five years, I recognized a dichotomy. Although I saw the shining steeple reaching for Heaven, it was the ironclad windows at street level that caught my attention. Those fortified windows seemed to be holding out the Devil. I knew I'd found what I'd been looking for. A place where I could define my style of ministering. I would use the love God had given me to find a way to reconcile this seeming schism."

A tingling of pride and reverence goes up my spine. Again, Sandra gives a little nod, as though she too understands. "I settled into my new environment. Setting up housekeeping, as it were." I chuckle, reliving in my mind how hard it was to find acceptable furniture in such a poor neighborhood. "And I actually became liked, if not loved, by the regulars in our church. In a predominately black neighborhood in America, there are many churches. The Catholic faith doesn't dominate as it does in some areas. Despite that, I set out to become a reformer of the community. I worked with groups from all denominations."

As I tell my story to Sandra, I realize how my love for God had actually strengthened despite the pitiful environment. God had taken me from the beautiful mountains and placed me in squalor. It was a compliment of the highest order. I was going to repay His faith in me. In His name I was going to change the face of the street I had seen upon arrival. I would fill that community with saved souls.

"I knew always that my love for God was returned," I told Sandra. "Even though there were heartbreaks and sorrows during my stay, He never deserted me. In repayment, I did all in my power to spread His word and save His souls."

I look to Sandra to see if she can fathom the depth of my love for God. I notice a slight tear sneak from her eye. She asks, "If you loved your work in that place so much, why did you leave?"

I realize that Sandra would have no inkling of the inner workings of the Church's hierarchy. At times, I think I also have no understanding. The term arrogant hierarchy is often applied to certain governments and very large corporations. It might be an apt term to describe all organizations that become large and are run by man. I have to agree with Sandra's quandary. If God had been in charge, He certainly would never have taken me from an area where I was doing so much good and where my heart was so full of love for Him. But, unfortunately, people seem compelled to change things when they are running most smoothly. I felt God, in His wisdom, gave mankind the right to rule themselves, however inanely they do so.

I don't explain all this to Sandra. It's not my place to put doubt in her heart. I simply say, "The Church felt that I had spent my time in Hell and so, as a show of thanks, I was transferred to this tranquil town. I knew about Monsignor Ramón's illness and that a replacement was needed." I chuckle as I add, "Although, I'm still not sure what a priest from the slums might add to this community. When I was forced to leave Detroit, I couldn't imagine how I'd ever again fit so neatly into God's plan"

Sandra looks at me with a quizzical frown. "Do you think God betrayed you by sending you here?" Her voice takes on a perplexed quality as she speaks. She's waving her arms around her to take in the whole of the small city in which we live. In confusion she adds, "How could you not love such a beautiful place?"

We start to jog again, knowing we have a destination to reach. Jim must be wondering what has happened to his hapless friend. Sandra and I seem to have a tacit agreement to jog slowly. This is to be our mutual nod toward exercise.

As we move down the trail, I answer Sandra as best I can. "I've often wondered how I truly feel about my move here. I think maybe the bishops and cardinals saw me more accurately than I did myself. They thought that in Detroit I was burning myself out and would soon be good to no one." I look toward Sandra to see if she understands. As she nods, I continue, "Even after I knew I was to be transferred, I never once lost my love for God. I felt, in some way, He was sending me toward a new challenge. Maybe a larger challenge. I relished the opportunity, even though I would be sad to leave the decayed community where I was doing so much good.

"Soon after I had first arrived in Detroit, I bought a very old car, one that would get me to and from those necessary meetings in my parish. I had to have a junk car, so I'd be on the same terms as my parishioners. When I was told I'd be coming here, I knew my

old car would never hold up to such a long trip, so I got rid of it." I
smile at the pleasant memory of that rattling and rusting car.
"Since I didn't have a suitable car for my journey here, I convinced
my sister that I needed her to drive me. Actually, that was just an
excuse to see her." My thought about how rarely I get to see
Maggie causes a sadness to come over me. "I love her so much.
And miss her dearly."

Chapter 8

As we jog along in silence, I wonder what Sandra is thinking. The fact that her earlier attitude was so sprightly and it has now become so serious worries me. I hope the new me doesn't always have this effect on women. I shake my head to clear it of nostalgic memories of Detroit. I need to focus on the present and what I might have said to change the behavior of this sweet and vivacious young lady.

She has already confessed to me that she was playing with my feelings, trying to tempt me toward a physical relationship. If I were so inclined, Sandra would undoubtedly be my first choice. Her soul is so nicely wrapped in an angelical and intelligent mind and body. With some foreboding, I find myself in absolutely unfamiliar territory. Being tempted like this is quite a novel feeling. I'm actually becoming obsessed with the possibility.

We round the last bend in the trail and head toward where I will be meeting Jim. Within five minutes or so, I'll no longer be with Sandra. If I hope to see her again, outside of mass, I must find a way to make sure such an event will happen. Years ago, I thought it was silly when my friends would agonize over how to successfully ask a girl out on a date. I now see it as an important survival mechanism. This is certainly a situation I've heretofore never been in. I haven't a clue what I'll say to Sandra. If there is a God, I'll let Him guide me. I'll let Him take over my tongue.

Sandra's silence comes to an abrupt end. "Father, again I'm going to say things as though I know what you're going through. It seems to me that everything you've said about losing the love of God has to do with your either leaving Detroit or coming to this town."

She's on a roll. At times a person will mentally get on a soapbox. I've learned in my years of counseling that it's best to let them continue. I've also learned from counseling that I'm better off not telling my parishioners what The Church, or even I, might think is right or wrong. And I've learned that if I ever do say what seems to me to be so obvious, it would do no good. Only if my parishioner comes to an understanding on his own will his behavior change. With these thoughts in mind, I say nothing. I pray Sandra will reach the same conclusion I've reached concerning the two of us. I would like her to also desire a relationship. Against all my previous beliefs and vows, I find myself not being concerned about saving Sandra's soul. I want her as a woman. A beautiful bundle of flesh and blood.

Sandra continues, "I just can't believe you would change a lifelong love of God just because I was sitting in your church."

Maybe I have it wrong. I thought she would try to justify her own thoughts and actions. Rid herself of any possible guilt by laying the blame elsewhere. But she's not telling me how she feels about having a relationship with me. She's not telling me that my romantic feelings are reciprocated. What a muddled mess.

Many times I've tried untangling a triangulated love affair. A wife, having an affair with her husband's best friend, telling me how madly in love she is with the other fellow but not wanting to hurt her husband. It seems that in Sandra's mind, God has taken on the part of the wronged husband. Apparently Sandra doesn't want to hurt God. I would laugh out loud at the thought except I think Sandra might find my humor warped and mean spirited. And I want her to think only good thoughts about me.

Sandra studiously jogs next to me. Her head is down as though she's trying to discern the composition of the asphalt. A sure sign she feels she's said too much. Jogging may take a lot of different abilities, but being studious is not one of them. Again I wish I knew for sure what she's thinking.

I see Jim sitting on a bench just ahead of us. He's with another jogger, chatting and patiently waiting for me at our appointed meeting place. He seems to be enjoying the day as he moves his hands in animated discussion. He certainly does have a way with words, but without his arms he'd be voiceless. I wave to him as I see that he notices me. As he waves back, I realize I need to quickly put Sandra's and my relationship to rights. I have about one minute before I lose my opportunity to speak privately with her.

"Sandra," I say with strength I don't feel. "I can't tell you what has caused me to lose my love for God." Even though I've recently begun to doubt my chosen profession, I lie to Sandra and say, "But I have no doubt that God exists." I won't burden Sandra with my doubts about God's existence. I don't want on my conscience that I've removed her hope for eternal salvation. I've begun to believe that the only lasting thing religion can give is hope. The hope of God's omnipotence. It's the hope of a better life that helps our society. Hope is a powerful weapon against tyranny and evil. I shan't do anything to harm someone else's hope.

"I don't think God has betrayed me in any way. In my heart, it just doesn't feel right. It's not some sort of betrayal that has me upset." I look intently at her as I realize how strongly I know I'm correct on this issue. I continue, shaking my head sadly. "I just don't feel toward God as I used to. I've lost my belief." I hesitate a moment before adding, "And my love."

Having satisfied my need to nurture another's hope, I now decide to change the direction of our conversation. If I don't move our conversation toward dating, I'll miss a wonderful opportunity to get to know this beautiful woman. I muster all my courage to try a tactic I've often heard will work wonders with women. Flattery combined with a plea for sympathy. In my heart I feel shamed by my ploy, but I rationalize that the prize is well worth some indignity. "I can't tell you how much I've missed a female relationship in my years of being a priest. And then I saw you in my church. And now I've met you and gotten to know you." I look her in the eye, hoping to hold her attention with my sincerity. "I'd love to go out with you. Socially." I chuckle nervously. "On a date." Then I add, "I've never asked a woman on a date before."

I watch for her reaction. Possibly a sparkle in her eyes or a glint of happiness. Or a brightening of her smile. It never appears. Sadly I realize I've said something that has made the proverbial light turn off. Somehow, in some way, I've blown it. I've said something that has swayed her away from being interested in me. She must have misinterpreted my invitation. Or my absolute naiveté is grating on her nerves.

Jim is saying his goodbyes to the other joggers as Sandra and I come to a stop near him. As I stand beside her, I wipe the sweat from my brow with my shirt and try in vain to catch my breath. Again I realize what horrible shape I'm in. Sandra is acting as though she just got out of bed after a restful night's sleep. No hard breathing and nary a trace of sweat. As I gulp air quickly so I can introduce her to my friend, I raise my head and try standing straight.

Jim says as he walks toward us, "I was worried about you. Thought maybe you'd been mugged. Or fallen over dead and were now sitting on the knee of your Lord." Big smile on his face. The man has no fear of blasphemy.

Before I can speak, Sandra holds her hand out to Jim as she says, "I'm sorry I kept the good Father from you. He's been waylaid by a wicked woman. I'm afraid I was acting out the role of a temptress while we were jogging." Between the two of them, they are having a grand time with my profession. I seem to have a penchant for befriending those who take their religion with some insouciance. It's as though these two were woven from the same pattern. No grave evil or salacious sin in their hearts. Thus they know any Supreme Being that might exist will take their lighthearted banter kindly. It's this very lightness of heart that makes them both attractive as companions.

I do my social bit. "Jim, this is Sandra. She's a parishioner in my church." I don't mention to Jim what Sandra and I have actually been talking about. "She agreed to slow her speed to match mine. I've been boring her with stories of my mundane existence before I came to your little hamlet."

Sandra throws me a mischievous little grin as I leave out all the important stuff that was said. I hope Jim doesn't notice her look. She says, "Father, nothing about you or your life seems mundane to me. But I have to be leaving the two of you here." She indicates a path that goes out of the park. As she gets ready to leave, I feel my spirit plummet. At this point, I'm so depressed at her upcoming absence, I don't care if Jim notices my mood.

Sandra continues, looking directly at me. "Father, something you said earlier intrigued me. Can I buy you lunch today so we can continue our conversation? I'll be at that cute restaurant down the street from your church at noon. You know the place? I think it's called the 'Satan's Cathedral' or something like that." More blasphemy, but I have to admit, appropriate for my current thinking.

In the blink of an eye my heart goes from the lowest of lows to soaring in the heavens. At times like this, I wonder how the sciences and those who think man is only flesh and blood can possible explain an instantaneous mood change such as I've just experienced. At lightening speed, even my aching thighs suddenly feel good. No chemical could possibly pass through my body in just an instant. Only a soul could react so quickly. My head is nodding numbly up and down. She could have said I should jump in the lake and I'd have agreed.

Then, as if to dampen my hopes, Sandra adds, "I'd like to discuss more concerning your recent loss."

Again I realize I have no experience with the workings of a woman's mind. I thought the conversation she eluded to was our getting to know each other. I thought she had taken me up on my invitation for a date. As I realize my mistake, my spirit again tumbles.

My optimistic side then comes forth. At the very least, I'll get to see her again. If I've made an etiquette error in asking her for a date, I'll have another chance. Holding on to that slight hope, I smile as I say, "Lunch would be fun. I'll meet you there at noon."

Jim is having a joyous time watching us. I'm sure he'll be rubbing my nose in every perceived particle of perversion. It's his way of proving his undying friendship toward me. Even realizing the hackling I'll be taking from Jim does little to dampen my hopes.

Sandra looks back as she jogs away, and says, "Oh, by the way. I'll be bringing a friend." With that she sprints off as though our earlier jogging had been a cakewalk.

Chapter 9

I pretend I'm still catching my breath as I lower my head and put my hands to my knees. I know if I look up, Jim will be giving me a devilish look. Before dealing with my friend's irritating wit, I have to bring my thoughts together.

Why is Sandra bringing a friend? Does she think I implied I wanted a sex orgy? Despite having lived a cloistered life, I've heard about the more outlandish sexual appetites of man, about sexual threesomes. And I know from years of giving confession that men and women actually participate in such activities. But I'm having enough trouble thinking about having sex with one woman. I haven't a clue what I'd do with two. I'm sure Sandra does not see me doing anything so foreign to my beliefs. It must be apparent to Sandra that my behavior this morning is as wildly sexual as I've ever been in my life.

It could be she is thinking she needs the protection of a friend, although she didn't act as though she was treading in dangerous waters. It's far easier for me to believe that Sandra finds me boring than that she finds me kinky. I convince myself that I've not so badly misread this young woman. She surely doesn't think me capable of things kinky or dangerous. She must be bringing a friend for an entirely different reason.

Now is not the time to be dwelling on this new and disturbing turn of events. I set the thought aside knowing I can't put Jim off another second. I raise my head as though I've just now caught my breath. I look his way. As I expected, he looks as though he's caught someone with his pants down. A mischievous smile, but also a hint of curiosity. Apparently his curiosity wins out over his need to provoke me.

"What was that all about?" That's all he can think of to say. My early morning behavior has apparently rendered my loquacious friend almost speechless. Rarely is an attorney at a loss for words. I will bless this moment.

Although the hour is early, the day has already been full of surprises. My behavior has startled even me. I don't know if I should be proud or ashamed of my actions. Times past, I would never have looked at nor spoken to a woman as I did today with Sandra. In the past, I had a love of God that couldn't be denied. My only thoughts about women were as souls to save.

A new sense of detached reality has been growing in me all morning. The strange conversation with Sandra has only enhanced the sensation. It's a vague feeling that something bad is going to happen. It's as though I'm waiting for the proverbial other shoe to fall. An air of unreasonable panic begins to fill me.

I see Jim reaching into the little fanny pack he always carries when we jog. I irrationally worry he's going to pull out a gun and shoot me. Put me out of my misery. Just as suddenly, I realize how ludicrous my thought is.

Instead, Jim removes his cell phone. As he unfolds the tiny device and pulls up it's antenna, he looks over to me and says, "You look like a man who wouldn't mind having someone to talk to. So, since I have no appointments this morning, I think I'll call my office and tell them I'll be late." I start to speak, intending to say it won't be necessary. He waves me off. "Hey, you've already made me late with your dilly dallying with every woman on the block." He's mocking me. But, with good humor. He turns away to speak into his phone, apparently explaining his absence to his secretary. He says his goodbyes and folds away his phone, placing it back into its pouch. Then he turns to me and says, "Let's get some exercise." With that he takes off at a fast pace.

I sprint to catch up. Sprinting is never a good thing for me to do. I'm immediately out of breath. I try to finagle my way out of additional jogging by appealing to Jim's love for physical activity. "I'm really sorry I took so long meeting up with you. I can understand if you'd like to run without me holding you back. Why don't you just go on ahead and we can touch base by phone when you want me to tag along with you on some other day."

Hidden deep in my heart is the hope that Jim will take the invitation and not jog with me. So I can dwell more about what might be brewing between Sandra and me. I also don't want to tell Jim what Sandra and I had been talking about. I'm muddled and befuddled. And I'd prefer that my friend Jim not know that. Or maybe it's all just an excuse so I won't have to maintain his fast pace.

As I pant and sweat to keep up, I realize that I'm expecting God to solve this latest problem for me. Maybe if I continue to run this fast, The Almighty will cause me to fall prostrate with a heart attack. Even though I have come to doubt God's existence, apparently my life long habit of putting myself into God's hands still exists. I've spent my life knowing God is omnipotent. I can't seem to shake this knowledge, despite the voice in my mind saying He doesn't exist.

Jim slows his pace so I might more easily stay astride. I give God the credit, as I thank Him for a respite. I try again to tell Jim it's okay if he takes off and runs without me, but he interrupts and starts to talk, asking about Sandra. He's intentionally frustrating my wish for solitude. He's apparently unwilling to let me off the hook so easily. Being Jim, he brings humor to the situation. "If I knew Catholic girls were so attractive, I would have converted years ago. You say Sandra is in your congregation?"

"Watch your wandering eye, my boy," I tease back. "Or else I'll be forced to tell Pam. I'm sure she would have a thing or two to say about such behavior." I'm referring to his wife. I was best man at Jim and Pam's wedding when he was still in law school. I knew they were both uncommitted to a specific religion. Humorously, I'd told them I'd be honored to officiate as their priest on the condition that they'd both convert to Catholicism. Of course, they refused. It's been somewhat of an ongoing joke amongst the three of us ever since.

"She wouldn't care. Your threats of causing me marital disharmony don't bother me at all, Father." He say's the last word with good-humored satire to emphasis our different religious affiliations.

Despite Jim and Pam never having been a religious couple,

they seem to be happy in their marriage. They are also raising a wonderful and decent young son. This isn't to say Jim has never had his rough moments in life. He has, but in my newly found self-absorption, I view Jim's past sorrows as very slight compared to my current distress. Upon recognizing my coldhearted attitude, I become even more disgusted with myself. It seems my empathy and compassion for other human beings has also deserted me.

I mentally compare how Jim and I have lived our lives. I've known for years how different belief systems can cause different life styles. But I wonder how an avowed agnostic like Jim can be so successful and happy? To a religious fundamentalist, Jim's way of life should ultimately bring fire and brimstone upon himself and his family. A more moderately religious observer would see Jim's success as evidence that God works in mysterious ways. And to those who have fallen away from religion, the answer is even easier. Their attitude would be that God, if He even exists, could care less what Jim and Pam do. This attitude of the disbelieving has always saddened me. Even now with my lack of faith, I feel a rush of remorse. Not having God's love fill my heart is becoming ever more difficult. I must find a way to pull myself together and resolve my spiritual vacuum.

Both Jim and I run along for a few minutes in comfortable silence. We each feel our own banter has surpassed the other's and each of us is now willing to leave our teasing at that. Putting aside my thoughts of Sandra, I begin to feel an internal peace. I'm satisfied enough with how my body is reacting to maintaining Jim's fast pace. All was well with the world. Then I hear the screeching of tires from a far away street. Suddenly, I feel exhausted.

"With all this exercise," I explain to Jim, "I feel a bit of a headache coming on."

Chapter 10

I try distracting my mind from my body's aches by reflecting on my friendship with Jim. How can I explain away my friend's happiness and success despite his agnostic attitude? Simply saying that God works in mysterious ways is much too easy. I know, though, with my newfound doubts about the existence of God, that Jim's life is an affront to my previous life choices.

Life had been easier when I hadn't doubted God. Having lost His love is bringing me a great deal of unhappiness and unease. And now, to make things worse, I wonder if I've wasted away my life. I also worry about my plan for a new life. Despite my wanting to fill the void with the love of a woman, I'll grieve my loss of God's love.

Jim again brings up the subject of Sandra. "I noticed it wasn't just me looking at the wiggle in those little shorts of hers. And that tight tee shirt." He says this gleefully. He was having a lot of fun with my feelings. "I've suspected it all these years. You actually do have male hormones racing through your blood stream." A mischievous glint is in his eye.

Jim immediately notices the distress his words are causing me. He slows his pace so I can more easily keep up. His eyes look at me with compassion. If I weren't so concerned with my own plight, I'd take this opportunity to regale my friend's normal unfeeling attitude and point out to him the advantages of a merciful demeanor.

He stops for a moment, and then looks at me with compassion as he says with feeling. "Tommy, what's going on? I'm not sure I've ever seen you looking so sad."

I think of Jim as a good friend. Usually our banter is what draws us to each other. There are those times, though, when we have shared our innermost thoughts. Last year, Jim was going through a tough time. When we'd get together, Jim would describe the sad state of his life. I knew from counseling my parishioners that I could never just look at the obvious trappings of a person's existence to know how they were feeling about their lives. Despite what seemed to be a hugely successful career and family, Jim felt he'd misspent the last ten years. He decided he'd blown it when he became an attorney rather than a rock and roll musician. Even though he was bright enough to realize very few honky-tonk musicians ever became rich or famous, he was sure the musician's life had been meant for him.

Then, a few months back, Jim got over his jaded attitude about life when he and a fellow attorney started their own small law practice. Apparently he only needed to go his own way, and not in the direction of some large corporate law firm. Since that time, I've not seen any signs of depression in him. Amazing what being in charge of your own life can do for your attitude.

As we continue to jog at a speed more to my liking, I wonder if it might help my current confusion and low level of confidence to confide in my friend. I take a chance. "I've wondered for a while now if there might not be more happiness in sharing my life with someone like Sandra rather than living the life I've been living."

Apparently my words are more startling than I could have imagined. Jim immediately comes to a halt as he keeps his eyes on mine. I stop running also. Standing there, looking at my friend, I realize my lousy mood is getting in the way of everyone's exercise. If I'd known before that all I had to do in order to get people to run less, and rest more, was to make such proclamations, I might have proclaimed more often about most anything.

"Father O'Malley. I realize that over the years I've poked fun at your profession. I always figured you took my joshing with humor---not seriously." He says somberly. Apparently Jim has the idea his teasing has influenced my changed attitude. Although he is correct in detecting a new slant on my life, I need to relieve him of any thought that he somehow contributed to it. My mood is not only causing both he and Sandra to lose exercise. They both also feel guilty, thinking somehow they've caused my current depression. I never expected my loss of faith to so adversely affect those around me. I need to find a way to stop being so self centered and to again be concerned about others.

"Don't get me wrong, Jim. This new thinking isn't something that's happened because of our friendship. Although I admit it happened about the time I left Detroit and came to this town." Jim gives me a dubious look, as though he thinks a man of my religious standing might lie to him. I continue, "In fact, my change of attitude is mostly what Sandra and I were talking about. It's what made our jogging go so slow."

I look guiltily toward the ground as I tell Jim how I'd lied to him. "Although she did want to know about Detroit, it wasn't my mundane life we really talked about. We mostly talked about our feelings for each other." I look up at him, saying, "I'm sorry I lied to you about that." He waves away any concern I might have, with a slight nod and a twitch of his nose. It's nice to have dear friends.

Again I think about unintended consequences. My doubting the existence of God has not only overwhelmed me with despair. In the last hour I've filled first Sandra and now my friend Jim with guilt. I've also ruined both Sandra's and Jim's workout. I can do something about that, at least for Jim. I start to jog. If he wants to hear my thoughts, he's going to have to keep up with me. I might feel guilt from my loss of love for God. I shan't also be guilty for causing both these good people to lose out on exercise.

Jim easily catches up with me and we again jog side by side. I look at him and say, "Over the years, you and I have had many discussions about God and the meaning of life. So I think you know how I've felt about God." Jim nods his head, so I continued, "Recently, though, I've come to wonder whether my faith hasn't been misplaced." My comment brings a frown to my friend's face. I quickly continue before he can interrupt. "I have no experience talking with a woman in the way I did with Sandra this morning. And as one would expect, our conversation didn't go well. What I wanted to tell her was I'd love to have a date with her." Jim's frown turns to shock. I put my hand up to ward off any comments. Soon enough he'll get his say. "I'm pretty sure I didn't communicate my intentions. I tried to tell her that since there's no longer a reason for me to be celibate, I'd love to entertain a relationship with someone like her."

Jim was very perplexed, his face showing extreme surprise and distress. Why is it that a man like Jim, who never doubts his own right to have a sexual relationship and family, is aghast at my wanting those things?

"Let me get this right. You actually suggested having sex with that young lady." I'm not sure if Jim's going to have a heart attack or keel over laughing. His face is turning many shades of color, ranging from dark red to purple.

"I wouldn't exactly say I mentioned having sex with her." This conversation is getting more difficult than I could ever have imagined. Also the traffic noise from the street is becoming bothersome and my headache is getting much worst. I'm having difficulty concentrating as we jog along the sidewalk next to the turbulent traffic and screeching tires. Despite my difficulties, I try to explain what's become baffling even to me. "I've never before doubted my life choices. Laypeople often think a priest is somehow sacrificing his own life in order to give himself to God. I've never felt any sacrifice. Until recently." As I speak, my headache worsens. The throbbing behind my forehead takes on a rhythm much like my feet on the pavement. I can't say whether the fumes from the cars are the cause or this confounded exercising. This has not been my best of jogging days.

"So, you've decided to give up the priesthood and start dating," Jim comments, waving his arms derisively toward where we'd last seen Sandra. "Her. Whatever her name is…Sandra?"

He's actually exasperated with me. An adult hasn't treated me like this since my parents admonished me for wanting to collect up all the homeless on skid row and take them to mass with us. I can't exactly say I got in trouble for the thought. But I knew from how Mom and Dad acted that such behavior was not something I was going to be allowed to continue. I'm getting a similar reaction from Jim concerning my recent thoughts about Sandra.

In the future, I'll have to change how I deal with people. In my new life, Sandra and I will need friends like Jim, and his wife and son. Maybe I'll have as much difficulty maintaining a friendship with Jim as I had in asking Sandra to entertain a relationship. It was all so much easier when I had God's love. Somehow I have to lead this conversation in a more positive direction. Thus far today, I've had very little luck leading any conversation effectively.

"I'm sorry you think so badly of Sandra. She really is a wonderful girl. Once you get to know her," I counter.

Apparently Jim worried he'd overreacted to what I've said. "Don't get me wrong, Tommy. I'm sure she is very nice. But if she steals you away from your one true love, I'm going to have to be convinced it's truly what you want." His concern is for me. He is truly a friend.

Then, his teasing demeanor returns as he adds, "And it'd better be more than just an interest in her well formed bottom." The lascivious smile returns.

Chapter 11

We round the last corner and head down the street toward the church. My thoughts are in a jumble. I've known for a while now that I've been on the cusp of a change. Even given that knowledge, the careening state of my emotions is unsettling. Much like what I'd imagine happens on a roller coaster ride. The lurch upward only to be followed by the sickening feeling of falling. Over and over again. This morning's ride on the mental roller coaster has been by far the worst yet.

As Jim and I come to a stop in front of my church, I try yet again to have Jim's sensible outlook on life help me untangle my thoughts. "Do you think a person's life can change significantly in only one day?" I ask.

I've said something to my friend that actually impacted him. His eyes take on that far away yet peaceful look. A look I've often seen when a person has taken the Lord into their heart. Knowing the spiritual leanings of Jim though, I know such a religious conversion is not what's happening here now. I wonder what Jim is thinking.

Jim slowly nods his head and gives a far away smile. "You bet," he says. "One day can become magical." He's apparently remembering such a day in his own life. I pray for a future that will bring me the obvious pleasure Jim's nostalgia is now bringing him. It's nice to know my friend has had magical moments.

Jim looks at his watch and then says, "I've pretty much blown the morning. How about if I buy you a cup of coffee at that Starbucks down the street?"

Since getting away from the disconcerting traffic, I notice my headache is diminishing. I check the time on my watch and notice it's not quite eight o'clock. I mentally organize my day. At ten, I have a baptism to perform but nothing until then. I rationalize that coffee might get the lingering cobwebs from my brain. So that I can more effectively play my part in a baptizing ritual my heart no longer can affirm. A nimble mind is needed, even in a fallen away priest. Coffee will certainly help.

"Sure. Maybe you can tell me how a day can become miraculous. God knows, right now I need a miracle." As I say this, I realize I am becoming ever more pitiful. If I don't change my ways, I'm going to become a whining self-loathing meager man.

Shaking my head to rid my mind of further pathetic thoughts, I fall into step next to Jim and say. "I apologize for my behavior today, Jim. I've just not been myself for a while now."

Jim seems to take my apology in stride. He smiles as he says, "As they say down under, no worries mate. I think having coffee is just the ticket. What you need is what you've been giving others for so many years. Hope. And I've got just the story for you. It proves good things can happen even to the likes of me." With that mystery hanging in the air, we jog toward Starbucks.

As we arrive at the store I remember the many times I've walked past this store but never gone inside. I admit I love a good cup of coffee. But something about a shop that sells so many types of coffee, with such exotic names, offends my senses. Apparently Jim doesn't share my concern. He approaches the store as though he's a regular customer.

As we enter I say, "I'm going to take you up on your offer to pay. I don't carry a wallet when we jog." I indicate with jocular derisiveness his "fanny pack."

Jim smiles and waves off my concerns as we approach the counter. "You mentioned once that you've never tried a latte. Now's your chance." When I nod my head in agreement, he places an order for two of the strange creamed coffees. As he pays, and then watches as they prepare our coffee I look around for a place to sit.

How can a coffee shop become so fashionable? I've heard it's because people bring their computers in and browse the

Internet as they get their morning shot of caffeine. I doubt this is the only reason. Yuppie coffee houses have been around for some time and seemed to do just fine even before the Internet became so popular.

As I wait for Jim, my mind takes up this new social puzzle. Being a priest has caused me to be somewhat insular, so I've had to work to keep in touch with the societal trends around me. I've noticed fads that come and fads that go. I'd just figured the popularity of Starbucks, and other such stores, were just another in a long line of short-lived fads.

The ongoing popularity of these establishments has proven to me how wrong I could be concerning mankind and society. I wonder if this might be the cause of my doubts concerning The Church and God. Maybe it isn't that I doubt God's existence. Only that I doubt my own abilities to perceive. Added to my loss of God's love is also a loss of confidence. That would certainly explain my current doldrums. But then, something doesn't feel quite right in my heart. Recognizing I've had a loss of confidence does nothing to quiet the voice in my head saying there is no God.

I watch Jim bring our coffee to the table where I'm sitting. I hope whatever story he has to tell will shake me out of my negative mood. I need to reestablish my self-confidence and rid myself of my self-loathing. I figure if coffee with Jim doesn't do it then surely my lunch with Sandra will. The thought of Sandra's sweet face causes my heart to swell. Then I remember that she's going to be bringing a friend. My opportunity to court her will again be delayed. As has happened all morning, just as my mood begins to soar something happens to cause it to plummet. Again I have the image of being on an emotional roller coaster.

Reaching for the coffee cup Jim hands me, I ease into the conversation he's promised. "So. You've experienced a life changing magical day?" I ask, adding humor to my voice. I don't need to spread my desolate mood.

"You remember when you first heard you'd be moving here from Detroit?" Jim begins, "And you visited Pam and me? On that visit you said that I didn't seem to be the cocksure guy you had known in college. Remember?"

I remember the visit with a smile, saying, "Yeah. A little

more than a year ago. My, time does fly, doesn't it?" Jim's mentioning that visit brings back my feeling of concern. I'd be leaving my parish in Detroit and the many dear friends I'd made. But my visit with Jim made me realize the good I could do in this community. Jim and his family made me feel welcome. I remember thinking though how much my friend had changed. He'd taken on a sad demeanor. I also remember thinking that if ever a man needed the wonders of the Lord, it was this man. In fact, it was my concern for Jim that made me realize how much I was needed in this town. Not only should the poor have hope, but also so should those that are well off. They also deserve something magnificent to look forward to.

I chuckle. "I trust I wasn't that hard on you. Cocksure? You're sure I used that description?" I'm trying to get some banter back into our conversation. I sip the whip cream laced coffee as I watch Jim using his tongue to get a gob of the cream off his upper lip. I smile saying, "This isn't bad, actually. Even if it isn't truly coffee. Though, you might want to clean it from your face."

He stretches his tongue and successfully licks his lip clean. Then smiles as he says, "You might not have called me cocksure, but I always felt you thought of me like that. And actually, I took it as a compliment. But at the time you visited us, I had become anything but cocksure." The sad smile crossing his face shows the inner despair of those troubling times. A remembrance of how bad his life had become. That he could go from that sad man of a year ago to this happy fellow today gives me some hope.

We continue to talk and enjoy our easygoing friendship. It's easy to see why I've always felt a fondness for this man. Being with him is changing my mood from sad depression to one of cheerful interest. What with our teasing each other about our selection of coffee and coffee houses, and his weaving a tale about his magical day, I'm feeling much better.

Jim tells me how his life had become boring and unhappy. Even, out of his control. Then, out of the blue, something happened. As he tells his story, I learn it was not so much that something had happened. More accurately, someone had happened. A new someone came into his life. In his case, the someone was a man named Roland, a new partner in the law firm where he was then working. I realize this is the very same Roland who is now Jim's partner in their recently started law firm.

I wonder if Jim is suggesting that Sandra will become my savior much as Roland apparently became his. That idea alone is enough to perk me up. A year ago, I would never have considered that a mere mortal man, or in my case a woman, could become a savior. The idea was blasphemous. "Savior" was a word reserved only for Our Lord.

My thoughts wandered toward my upcoming luncheon date and what Sandra might have in store for me. Is she bringing a friend to convince me of the wonders of a happy marriage? Perhaps a happily married friend she knows? The thought of having a family with Sandra brings a small smile to my lips. But, surprisingly, not the happiness I would expect such a thought to elicit.

Maybe her friend is a lover Sandra has hidden away. And he's going to tell me to keep my dirty thoughts and ideas to myself. With this thought, and with a sudden feeling of guilt, I stealthily look around the café. I worry that others might be able to see the filth flowing through my mind.

I've experienced shame before. But shame connected to sexual thoughts is new to me. Since I've never before experienced these desires that are being aroused by Sandra, I'd never before known the sordid guilt I'm suffering now.

I bring my attention back to Jim and his story. The humor and antidotes he adds to his tale have given me many minutes of joy and pleasure. More than just joy and pleasure. He relates his miracle day as a parable, and has given me some hope.

I see in Jim's eyes and his many smiles how he came back from the brink. He tells the story of how, with the help of his wife and son, he and Roland collaborated on that day to get the information that would save Roland from possible criminal prosecution. In the end, Roland became a close friend of the family. And also Jim's business partner. Shortly thereafter, Roland and Jim bolted from their corporate law firm and started a small firm of their own. As Jim sees it, on that day many great things happened to both him and his entire family. The ripple effect of that day not only changed Roland's life for the better, but also the life of Jim's wife and son. Roland had been the catalyst that changed Jim's life.

All in all, Jim's story invokes a sense of optimism. The humor and anecdotes he adds to his tale give me an anticipation of a bliss I've missed dearly. I can see in Jim's eyes how he had come back from the brink. Here was a story that could invoke hope in the most hapless. Perhaps his story will form the basis for a future sermon. As is my habit, I often use tidbits in life to create a sermon.

Why am I thinking about future sermons? Why am I still planning my future as a priest? I wonder how in the future I'll break these long time habits. Realizing how deeply ingrained are my clerical habits, and wondering what new habits will I have to develop for my new career? It makes me wonder at the difficulties I will face when I'm no longer a priest. Jim apparently has the same thought.

"Have you thought what you might do if you actually turn your back on your faith and your profession?"

Chapter 12

Jim's question startles me. Although my mood has had its ups and downs today, generally my spirit has been improving since coming in for coffee. Now he wants me to think about consequences of my new attitude. It's not as though I've had a history of being frivolous. Something about his question, and my situation, seems unfair.

Until recently, I've not been one to wallow in self-pity. Looking back at my life, I realize I've had no reason to dwell in such dark areas of my soul. I had a deep and abiding love for our Lord to console me from an early age. I knew, with that love to guide me, I would do well in a world sorely in need of help. I never really had the time to dwell on life's obstacles.

I've always known that by giving to others I had created in myself a serene happiness. As Jim continues to wait for my answer, I acknowledge to myself how important that aspect of my work has always been to me. Helping others has been my mainstay. And, despite my loss of faith, it is still as important as ever. Just because there isn't a God doesn't suddenly make our fellow man less important. The lack of a God doesn't mean I can't still find a way to lend a hand to others.

"It would have to be something that could help people in some way. Maybe some form of counseling." I suggest. I really have no idea what an ex-priest could do for work. In the past, I've often counseled parishioners through the turning points in their lives. These turning points often have obstacles. I will now have to deal with similar obstacles in my own life.

Jim and I chat a bit more about what type of occupation I

might find satisfying. His ongoing enthusiasm is encouraging. I'm quite sure he finds fault with what I've been saying. I can tell he's concerned about the direction my new life will be taking. Yet he's said nothing negative. I find his friendship endearing.

Realizing I still have obligations, including a baptism at ten, I look at the wall clock to confirm how late I'm getting. Jim notices my look and says, "That's right, you have something to do yet this morning, don't you?"

As I stand, I say, "Yeah. I need to be getting back and cleaned up. The Taylor's are bringing their new baby boy in to be baptized." I smile as I add, "Even though I might not be wearing the uniform much longer, I do think the Taylor's would find fault if I show up in my jogging shorts rather than my vestment."

We get up together to leave. Jim lightly grabs my shoulder to get me to turn toward him. Still smiling but now with a hint of concern in his eyes, he slowly asks, "What time will you be having lunch with Sandra?"

"I'm suppose to meet her in that restaurant right there." As we exit the coffee shop, I point across the street to the place Sandra had said she'd be lunching. "She said she'd be there at noon or so. Why?" I ask.

"Do you know when you'll be free this afternoon?" He smiles more widely. Although I detect the hint of a frown. "I'm mighty curious about this mystery woman who's trying to seduce my good friend to the dark side." He emphasizes the last two words, indicating a sinister fate.

I realize Jim is just teasing me and trying to get my goat. Nevertheless, I feel a shiver go up my spine. I shake off what might be a premonition of doom. Or it could be a prognostication of something much brighter. I prefer the sunnier vision.

Jim continues, "What say we meet later this afternoon. I'll call Pam and tell her I'll be late. I'm sure she won't mind if I buy you a baptismal glass of wine."

I laugh at my friend's lack of knowledge about my faith. "Wine is only a part of the sacrament of Communion," I say. Despite his joking with me, I realize Jim is being a friend and is truly concerned about my welfare. I'm touched. "Okay," I concede. "But it'll have to wait until six o'clock or so. I have to work on my sermon this afternoon." Again I realize how absurd it is to worry about my responsibilities if I will soon be leaving The Church. Duty dies slowly.

"Alright. Six it is," says Jim. "I'll be by to pick you up at the rectory." With that, he starts jogging away toward his neighborhood. He looks back and gives a wave.

Turning toward the church, I decide I too should jog home. As I start to get my rhythm, I realize how very sore my muscles became as I was having coffee with Jim. Slowing to a walk, I rationalize that I'm being sensible not to cause my body any injury.

I notice a bit of a bounce edging into my step as I begin to look forward to today's luncheon. I wonder what the next few hours might bring. I guess talking with Jim was actually therapeutic.

I like to think I'm good at counseling people and helping them to see their problems. But as with most people, it's much easier for me to see what's going on with another. I have no idea what's going on with me. I have nothing but confusion concerning my current dilemma. Probably Jim is more able to see me than I see myself. I wonder why he wants to get together later today over drinks. It must be a reluctant nod toward the new me. I'm sure he wants us to remain friends, even if I will be this new personality that is actually capable of making drastic life altering changes.

The only people who will call me Father in the future will be my own children. What a strange and wonderful thought that is. An image almost forms in my mind of Sandra and me and our two children sitting quietly in a living room as we read. I will still be a father, I think lightly.

I sigh as I realize I will still have the title of "Father," but I will have lost the love of all those other people who had once called me "Father", as their priest. The actuality of losing the love of all those other people hits me.

I can understand Jim's reluctance to embrace my new life. Since I implied to him that all my new attitudes had only just begun this morning, I can understand why he wouldn't give his immediate support. I knew I'd been thinking about this change for weeks now. This morning's meeting with Sandra was but a catalyst in an already occurring reaction. When meeting with Jim this afternoon, I'll explain how deliberate my actions in the last few weeks have been. I'll be able to show him that my life will be much happier as a layperson. This afternoon, I'll have the opportunity to explain everything to him. After what I'm praying is the beginning of Sandra's and my new life together.

I begin to daydream about afternoons to come. Outings with Jim's family and mine. The picture that has been forming in my mind takes on more substance as though it's coming alive. I envision pleasant afternoons sharing picnic lunches with Jim and his wife and boy. My kids playing with his son.

The idea that I too might one day have a family becomes surreal, even shocking. Possible even scary. Until today, I'd never thought of myself as being a father to only my own children.

With such thoughts clogging my mind I enter the ornate doors to the church. I see the Monsignor straightening up the alter and replenishing the votive candles. Hearing me enter, he turns and with a smile broad across his face, says, "My boy. There you are. I'd become convinced all that exercise had finally done its job and sent you to your final reward."

Guilt quickly crosses my mind as I realize I hadn't informed my Monsignor that I'd be a bit late due to stopping for coffee. But, as I see his impish smile, I begin to smile also. He knows I will carry out all my duties and he's just having his fun with me. "Nope. I decided to run around the lake a couple times for you," I tease. "I've decided I need to exercise for you as well as for me. So, I took my time and did double duty."

His quick response proves this little man enjoys the joking and jibing we often share. He continues in the same jocular vein, "I can tell by the limp in your gait that you certainly ran a long distance." Then he takes on a more serious demeanor. With sincerity he adds, "How are you doing, Tommy my boy?" His hand going to my shoulder emphasizes the depth of his concern.

Again guilt sweeps through me. This time, it has nothing to do with my tardiness. I know I should be telling this wonderful man my thoughts about leaving the priesthood. I've never thought myself a coward before. If I continue to act how I've been acting, I might have to revamp that view of myself. I put off answering by looking at my watch. Then say, "I'm fine. Thanks. I stopped for coffee with Jim and now I'm running a bit late for my ten o'clock baptism."

As I turn to leave, I can tell by the look in his eyes that I haven't completely convinced him. He might not know the full truth of what I'm contemplating but he knows something is amiss. He handles the situation like the truly decent man he is. His wisdom and perceptive eye show with his next comments. "I understand, Father O'Malley." His formality emphasizes how important he feels his comments are, and that I should take heed. "But if you ever do have something you need to talk about, I'm always here to listen." Then, his parting shot, again filled with humor. "As long as you make sure you rid yourself of that awful stench of sweat." The twinkle returns to his eyes as he goes back to placing new candles on the stand.

I hastily move toward my room in the rectory. I have twenty minutes to shower and get ready to bring a young child into The Church. As I enter my room and sit on the side of the bed removing my shoes, I worry whether it's acceptable to baptize a child into a belief I myself doubt. It was all so much easier when I had my abiding love for God. To lose that love, and the faith that went with it, has certainly caused me confusion. I toss my jogging shoes and shorts into a pile by the closet. Donning my robe, I head toward the shower.

Chapter 13

Hanging my robe on the hook behind the door reminds me of the many times I've fantasized about the similarity between my white bathrobe and the robe like vestments and sashes I wear while attending to my priestly affairs. Except for the difference in the degree of elegance and in the colors afforded a priest's attire. At times I have trivialized the rituals of the Church, letting an insouciant nature overtake my normally conservative manner, I've considered purchasing different-colored bathrobes so they will match the cassocks I wear on any given day of the week. In that way, both my private and public attire will correspond to the days in the life of Christ. A ridiculous bit of rebellion I have always overcome in the past. My new worry is that I will become overwhelmed by these absurdities in the future.

In times past, I've been concerned that the rituals of the Church might actually get in the way of hope and faith—that the rituals might actually come between a person and his Savior. It troubles me that some rituals, such as different colored robes, might do more harm than good. Usually though, I've fallen into step with the Church's beliefs and felt the sacraments and the rituals of the Church can help guide a person toward salvation. These warring thoughts of a lifetime are going to be difficult to discard. Given that my future will be devoid of any faith in Christ, I now fear the rituals are only an exercise in hopelessness. And devotion to a non-existent God can be the cause of a wasted life.

With these ridiculous and unworthy feelings wandering aimlessly through my mind, I crawl into the shower. I envision the warm water washing my despair into the sewer, much as it is washing my sweat down the drain. My silly views are being washed away. Abandoning my thoughts of colorful robes in my closet, and hopelessness of the faithful, I again turn my attention to Sandra.

I begin to wonder about my future. A year from now, might I be in a shower much like this shower, except in a suburban neighborhood? With my dear sweet wife humming merrily in the kitchen as she cooks my breakfast? Since such feelings are so foreign to my thinking, I'm not completely sure if I'm choking up out of fear or the wave of love for another. I avoid this latest dilemma in my mind. I rapidly finish my scrubbing and exit the shower.

As I dry my body, I think back to times in my past when terror had overcome me. There was that time when I was working in the little church in the mountains and one of my parishioners took me skiing. I think the man was using the outing, as payback for what he perceived was a slight from God.

Upon arriving at the ski slope, he first made sure I could stay upright and on my feet while wearing skies. Then he convinced me that I should slide down a hill from the top of the mountain. As I remember it, he said in a lilting Irish brogue, "Don't worry man. It's but a bit of a hill. We call it a green run which means you can go as fast as you want."

I should have been bothered by the mischievous glint in his eye. At the time, I felt positive that an Irishman would never do harm to another of his ilk. With hardly a nudge, I began to slide. Downhill. Fast.

I can remember his chortling getting fainter and fainter behind me as I miraculously stayed on my feet, yet continuing to gain speed. The terror became intolerable as the speed increased.

Soon thereafter, my Irish tormentor actually confessed his sin. For all I know, he's still reciting his Hail Mary's. I spared no sympathy as I handed out his penance. It was only my absolute faith that I'd be saved by God that had kept me emotionally sound.

I don my bathrobe and head again toward my bedroom. I realize I no longer have that abiding faith in God to guide me. I'll have to find my own way through the turmoil I now feel. Having loved only God, I never imagined that thinking about a physical and emotional bond with another human could bring such anxiety. Yet thinking about Sandra does just that. I enter my bedroom and begin to cloth myself. I wrench my mind from what is becoming an uncomfortable topic, the topic of Sandra.

I'm much more comfortable thinking about something familiar such as the upcoming baptism I'll be performing. The child's name is Tommy. Same as mine. I smile wondering if he too will go through childhood and adulthood being called Tommy. In my case, Tommy was the nickname that had mercifully been bestowed on me by my sister. She didn't like my Christian name. From an early age, I was only called by my given name, Thomas, when I was in trouble. It was that negative reinforcement, for the name my parents had bestowed on me that encouraged me to favor my nickname. I've often thanked my sister for not thinking of me as a Thomas even though I'd been named after one of the Apostles.

At my own baptism, when I was only a babe in the arms of my father, the priest would have uttered my Christian name. I've since thought that God preferred to think of me as Tommy and not Thomas. It's why I never felt morally wrong, even as a priest, when I preferred my nickname to the good Christian name. God would never consider this a lapse. It had been God's doing that inspired my sister to argue against my parents when they demanded I be called Thomas.

"A good Christian name," they maintained. "A name used often in the Bible," they said. "And look at the saint's since the crucifixion, who have borne that good name," they ended. Since I was still an infant, I had no say in the matter. But my sister has told me, repeatedly, that I owe her. Her battles with my mother and father over my nickname have become family lore. She insisted I would become some sort of geek and socially unacceptable if I were forced to be a Thomas my whole life.

Of course, the word geek had not yet come into common use. In those days, I'd have been a nerd. Same animal. The high tech economy spawned a new name for a nerd. Geek now describes that antisocial, book mongering, broken spectacle wearing, unlovable, and unloving individual. The name changed but the description has stayed the same. I thank my sister for saving me from that fate and all that ridicule.   Growing up as Tommy allowed me to go my own way. Even though many of my schoolmates did consider me antisocial, and book mongering. I never wore spectacles, broken or otherwise. As for being unlovable and unloving, I had God.

I put on pants and a shirt that will be acceptable for my lunch date with Sandra. Then I cover my clothes with a cassock and head toward the baptistery through the atrium. As I walk past, I glance at the grandfather clock as I pass it and realize it's two minutes before ten. I won't be tardy for Tommy's special day.

As I walk from the rectory, I think about the infant whom I'll soon meet. Unlike when I was born, parents today have the sense to give names that might stick to their children. Tommy is this child's Christian name, not a nickname.

Once again, the pang of my lost love for God hits me. In the past, I would have felt that the ceremony we will soon share would allow young Tommy to have the happiness that a love of God and Church can bring. I would have hoped that by baptizing Tommy, I'd bring another child into The Church. So that one day in the future he might also don the collar and bring hope to the masses. I might even have visualized this young babe taking an elevated position in The Church's hierarchy, where he could offer food to the starving and comfort to the hurting. Where he might help rid the world of misery by bringing peace and prosperity.

I approach the chancel and look up at the alter. The statue of Jesus seems to be looking down at me accusingly as if to ask how I can be such a hypocrite. I envision him beseeching me by saying, "For God's sake man, have the gumption to at least practice what you preach. If you truly doubt the existence of God, at least have the courage to walk out. Don't propagate that which you doubt."

I study the statue of The Lord. He who, until recently, was my Savior. Such words as I've imagined him saying would never have actually left the lips of Jesus. At least not the Jesus I knew. Only recently has my mind dwelt on such sacrilege.

Stories abound about being possessed by the devil. Although I've heard of personal encounters with Satan, I've never before had such a confrontation. I have wondered about the underhanded ways in which Satan deals out his poison. And, I've wondered how I'd measure up to Satan's temptations. Is it possible I'm only being tested? Is the Black Angel just tempting me with the visions of Sandra?

I've been trained in the rituals used to exorcize a person of an evil spirit, although I've had concerns about this aspect of my chosen profession. The few times I've actually done an exorcism, I've doubted that I did anything to help. This is one of those uncertainties I've had to deal with concerning my church's creed.

I do believe the devil can possess man though. One needs only to look closely at mankind to see the working of original sin. The fact that sin exists has never been in doubt. My doubt would only creep in when I would perform an exorcism. In my experience, there was no apparent change in the person's behavior after I performed the ceremony.

The enemy of mankind's happiness is not in question. It is the devil. The question is only the technique used to rid man of his original sin. I've always believed that a more effective technique for ridding man of evil is needed. A technique that will actually free a person of those devils that haunted him. Since I have doubted my ability to purge the devil from man's soul, my method of ministering had been to give hope to my parishioners. I would give hope, yet always press them to overcome temptation with the use of discipline. I would also provide comfort with the use of consistent rituals. A rite is predictable thus reassuring.

Recognizing that it might only be Satan's insidious work that I've been hearing in my mind helps me to clear my thoughts as I prepare for the ceremony I'm about to perform. As are my parishioners, I'm reassured by the familiar. Performing the well-known steps of preparing for the upcoming baptism gives me relief from the emotions I've been struggling with.

I walk into the apse to collect those items I'll need for the upcoming sacrament of baptism. I gather my implements, first placing the basin and holy water onto the baptismal font. I gather up the ceremonial cloth I'll use to dry the baby's forehead and bless the child. With each step I take, I get a stronger sense of relief from my earlier doubts.

How can I doubt the good I can do as a spokesman for God? With so much misery in the world, surely someone must muster hope. These people are putting their faith in me to be their link to

God. If I'm able to bring comfort to this young family, how dare I doubt myself? And doubt God?

With resolve, I hold my head high. I am the smiter of evil. I bring hope and happiness to humans. I will overcome the workings of the devil and ignore the voice I hear in my head. There is a God. I'm sure of it. Despite the doubts I harbor.

I hear the door swing open and look up to see Tommy's parents. Tommy is in his mother's arms.

Chapter 14

With my love for God and The Lord's Church somewhat reaffirmed, I watch as the Parsells enter the chapel. I also recognize Bill's brother and Peggy's sister who are apparently to be the godparents. The Monsignor has told me the history of both families. Bill and his young wife Peggy have been members of this congregation since the seventies when they were both infants. The two families had always been close. So it was no surprise when five years ago, Bill and Peggy got married in this very chapel. The religious history of these delightful people strengthens my resolve. I am determined to put the voice of the devil out of my mind. It's my duty to give this young couple and their baby the comfort and continuity of church and community. It's the lifeline of a successful marriage. I must rise above my devils.

Smiling, I hold out my hand to Bill as the group nears the alter. "Hi Bill," I say. My first order of business is to put Bill and Peggy at ease. I then shake hands with his brother. I've often wondered whether to offer my hand to a woman. I've recently decided the modern thing to do is to offer my hand to all. In my youth, shaking a woman's hand wasn't much done. I've found that if I do shake hands with an old-fashion woman, she won't be offended. But, not shaking hands with a modern woman often brings wrath. In this instance my quandary is solved for me. Between the purse hanging over Peggy's left shoulder and the infant Tommy squirming in her arms, any hope of a handshake is impossible. Peggy's sister is helping her handle the load.

I nod and smile toward them both, saying, "Peggy. Sally." Then looking at the bundle in Peggy's arms, my heart swells, "And I presume this is Tommy?"

One of the great rewards I've had in my years as a priest has been the baptizing ceremony. The look of pride in the parents' eyes has often brought me nearly to tears. It is no different now. With obvious joy, both parents say, "Yes." We all smile down at the little one as he stops wiggling and snuggles closer into his mother's arms.

I've noticed, through the years that sometimes those moments before a baptism can turn awkward. Mankind seems to make rituals out of the most common acts. My experience has shown that nervousness can be resolved by turning those few moments before the baptism into another sort of ritual. One that will bring the whole group together by giving everyone something in common. The comfort in any ritual is knowing exactly what to expect. I reach down to young Tommy's chin and mumble, "Goochie goo" as I lightly tickle his neck and under his chin. I'll admit this is a silly sort of ritual. And, not a ritual in the formal use of the word. Certainly it's not a ritual taught in the seminary. But my little self-implemented practice achieves its purpose of relaxing everyone. It also brings Tommy into the ceremony. I've often used this and similar ploys to involved an infant in their own baptism. As though he's already become familiar with this particular custom of tickling his chin, Tommy opens his eyes. Focusing on my face, he gives me the widest of smiles. My heart soars. Apparently so do the hearts of the parents and godparents. Seeing the reaction of these adults gives me faith that Tommy will be surrounded by love in his life.

As I've realized many times before, as long as I'm a priest I'll never need to be a parent. I'm already the Father to hundreds of children. I guide them to Salvation. I see them through their toughest trials. And I get the rewards of their beautiful smiles. A thousand times over. My love for God is unparalleled. What have I been thinking these last few days and weeks? How could I not love God? With a renewed feeling of God in my bosom, I feel peace. I hold my head high. Looking at the young family, I say, "Well. Lets get started."

Some people are unfamiliar with the baptism ceremony. They seem not to know what to expect or where to stand. So I gently yet firmly use my arm to guide their bodies to where they should stand. This particular problem doesn't occur today. These four people are familiar and comfortable in our surroundings. Their lifelong familiarity with our house of worship is evident. They each easily step to the appropriate places next to the alter. They seem fully familiar with what will take place, even knowing about the baptismal font holding the holy water. I suddenly realize that of course they are comfortable in this place. As babes, each in their turn had been in this exact ceremony in this exact chapel. And as each of their younger siblings was baptized, I have no doubt they also attended those. They've undoubtedly attended more baptisms here than I have. With the godparents standing to the side, Peggy keeps Tommy in her arms, her husband standing near her side. In this way, the father is also an integral part of the ceremony.

In the Detroit dioceses I would often correlate how a family responds during a baptism to how that family deals with everyday life. Not surprisingly, the more both parents involve themselves in the ceremony, the better that family seemed to cope with the impoverished neighborhood. I'm finding the correlation is equally true in a well to do environment. I'm optimistic that Tommy and his young parents have a high hope of success as a family.

I don the dark purple collar and start to recite the Latin chant. I've always preferred the ceremonies done in Latin. Call me old fashion. I continue to think ritual is the essence of our religion. That the priest is the interpreter of and communicator to God allows sanctity. I believe the cause for the multitude having fallen away from The Church is found in allowing the liturgy to be performed in the mother tongue rather than Latin. To this day, I believe Latin to be the language of The Church. Although I no longer have the blessing of the Church's hierarchy in my beliefs, I do strongly believe that Mass in Latin is necessary. This tenet is validated since only a priest, with his training, would understand the meaning behind the Latin chants. It provides an ethical elevation in its priests. Only a priest may communicate with God.

In requiring Latin during its rituals, the Church would allow priests to lead the way. The parishioners would naturally follow them into the heart of The Savior. The Latin language worked wonders for The Church for centuries. I find it odd that the upper hierarchy cannot understand why people are falling away from our religion in droves. For me, the answer is obvious.

I near the end of the ceremony, saying, "I baptize you in the name of The Father, and of The Son, and of The Holy Spirit." I hold young Tommy over a basin, and lifting the baptistery, I pour the holy water three times on his head. I begin making the sign of the cross over him. Young Tommy immediately starts to stir as the cool water touches his forehead. Rarely is an infant not somewhat startled at this point in the ceremony. It's to be expected. But as a young mother, Peggy has been taken by surprise. She immediately starts to fumble with Tommy as his wiggles become more insistent. One of my primary duties in the ceremony is to smooth all rough edges and make a memorable occasion seamless. I reach out to steady the child. I continue the sacrament which will bring a dying, and then a rising again, this time with Christ. All this with the single purpose of ridding young Tommy of every trace of original sin.

But Tommy seems intent on another action. His squirming turns to wild twisting. Both parents become involved in saving their son from an eminent fall. Bill reaches to retrieve his son from his wife's arms just as her purse falls from her shoulder. The resulting sounds echo as the contents from her purse hit the hard floor, bringing us all to silence. Even Tommy. He looks startled, as though he's created the commotion. Then Peggy moves into action. She goes to her knees to reclaim her purse's contents. She's obviously upset by this turn of events and noticeably near tears. "I'm sorry. I'm so sorry," she repeats over and over.

I fear she will begin to think she's prevented her son's original sin from being washed away. I begin to speak to her so I can put her concerns to rest.

But Bill takes over. To his wife he says, "That's okay, honey. Please don't let it upset you." He looks over toward me with an apologetic smile on his face and then continues to utter comforting words to his frantic wife. "It's just a little accident."

His words cause a slight shudder to go through me. I know I should also be uttering words of reassurance to Peggy. But instead, I begin to feel deadened. Since Peggy seems to be controlling her emotions, I rationalize that I'd do more harm than good by butting in. Bill continues to mutter small platitudes to his wife as I try to rid myself of my encroaching numbness. I prepare to finish the final step of the ceremony. I need to finish by making the sign of the cross over Tommy, thus imparting to him his new heart.

Peggy continues to gather her belongings, placing them back into her purse. As she continues her task, I wonder about the sacraments. In the past, I've found the sacrament of baptism to be the most comforting of the seven. That the old heart of stone and spirit die during this sacrament has to be one of the greatest gifts given by God. Also, at this moment the new heart is blessed, the door to our church and to Christ's heart is opened. Another special gift given by God. Although, feeling my headache pounding, I'm not as concerned about the gifts given by God at this moment, as I am with those things dealt by the Devil.

Despite my earlier promise to ignore the devil's tongue, Peggy's little accident seems to have rekindled my doubts. What if there is no God and the heart of Tommy was never made of stone? What if I'm only giving meaningless words to ward off the terrors of death? A death, which will only end a meaningless life? As my concerns intensify, so does my headache. The headache that has often accompanied my uncertainties these last few months.

Peggy finishes picking up her items and places them into her purse. Her sister helps her back to her feet. Peggy looks at me, and with an embarrassed smile says, "I'm so sorry, Father. Please forgive me."

I hastily try to comfort her. Having found that nothing succeeds in such circumstances like a little humor, I say, "Don't worry Peggy. The little bit of holy water that has hit the floor was needed to keep the termites at bay." Thank goodness for the decency of those around me whenever my attempt at comedy falls so flat. Everyone chuckles lightly. Even young Tommy has a big smile.

As Bill steps forward, now holding his child in his arms, I continue the washing away of original sin. I recite the last of the liturgical ritual and make the sign of the cross over the head of little Tommy. This time he's content to fall asleep during the rite of passage.

Chapter 15

As I bid a farewell to the Parsells, I wonder about the sin I may have just committed. The conundrum of performing a sacrament while also believing, there is no God to care, is perplexing. How can there be a sin if God doesn't exist? If there is no God, why then do I feel I've sinned? I often hear it said that God works in mysterious ways. I only hope He gets His act together and gets busy. I need some work here. I need a miracle, even if it is mysterious. Today's emotional roller coaster ride has left me nauseous.

Walking to the west end of our large church, I share inconsequential chatter with Bill and Peg. The pleasant chatter with this delightful couple helps to bring the throbbing of my forehead some relief. Young Tommy is again happily cuddled in his blankets, none the worst for the water dropped on his forehead. His mother and father have weathered the little incident during the ceremony and are again in bright spirits. It's only me that is feeling derelict. If it weren't for this confounded headache I'd be fine. I open the large ornate doors to let my parishioners leave and bid my farewells.

I return to the baptistery to neaten up after the recent ceremony and then look to my watch to see the time. Remembering my luncheon date with Sandra, and realize I'd better hurry if I have any hope of her thinking of me as a responsible and worthy mate. As I quickly walk back into the chapel, I wonder if I should cancel my luncheon with Sandra. Even if I do have romantic intentions, letting her see me when I have such a headache certainly won't show me to be worthy.

Out of nowhere an image of Sandra's smiling face fills my mind. Remembering the pleasant time I had with her this very morning, I resolve to ignore my headache. After all, earlier today when I ignored the words from the devil that were swirling in my mind, it seemed to put me back into a mood to believe there might be a God. Surely a headache is much more easily ignored than the devil's chant.

My step quickens and my movements become more focused as I store the baptismal artifacts into the cupboards in the apse. I head toward my room to prepare for the upcoming lunch date, removing my robe as I walk. Walking past the stairway I again encounter Monsignor Ramón moving slowly down the stairs. "How did the baptism go, my boy?" He asks. As always there's a twinkle in his eye and a smile on his face, despite his obvious pain.

His very presence brings lightness to my heart. I vow not to burden this wonderful man with my wavering ways. He'd never understand having one's faith shaken as mine has been of late. How could a man so pure of heart ever worry about God's existence?

His next statement shakes me to my core. With seriousness I've never before seen him display, he puts his arm around my waist and leads me toward a church pew. When I begin to pull away, his grip strengthens. He lightly says, "Come, my boy. I have a story I need you to hear."

"But, sir. I have a luncheon date." I look to my watch as if to verify how late I am and how right I am to resist him.

"I'm sure she'll wait." He smiles up at me. How did he know I was to have lunch with a woman? He looks at me sincerely as he says, "It's not a secret, you know? God already knows. And no one else matters." His serene smile will not be denied. He continues to insist on my coming with him. "I'll take but a few minutes of your time. Tommy." He continues to lead me gently but firmly down the aisle. "Father O'Malley. You're a good man. An honorable man. One of the most honorable I've had the privilege to work with in all my years." He chuckles, then says, "And believe me, there have been many men, and far too many years."

His cancer-ridden body takes on a strength that doesn't allow any argument from me as he pressures me to sit down. I'm sure if he were taller, the arm would be around my shoulders, or possibly my neck. The pressure in the small of my back does the job. I am forced to relent and sit.

"I'll not be surprised if you become shocked with what I'm about to tell you. But I've something important I want you to know right away. I've come to terms with what I'm about to tell you. The love of our Maker and the confessionals of our Church have enabled me to rise above my earthly weaknesses."

As we sit on a pew in the center of the Church, he bows his head. At first I think his head is bowed in shame but then realize he's thinking. Or praying. Curiosity takes over. I become very interested in what's so important for him to tell me.

He starts slowly, as he looks into my eyes and into my very soul. "It started a year after I left the seminary, during my first assignment." He continues to speak slowly, choosing his words. "I was assigned to a wonderful little parish in the South. I'd never before been to the South, but quickly fell in love with the small town where I'd been moved.

He shakes his head as if to remove the memories that seem to be flooding in. I know from experience how easily one can be side tracked from confronting difficult subjects. Despite the Monsignor's declaration that he's come to terms with this chapter of his life, I have a feeling he still finds some difficulty in speaking of it.

"I was lucky to have been assigned to a wonderful mentor in that undeveloped area of the country. His name was Father O'Connor." As Monsignor Ramón speaks, his eyes brighten with a thought. "You Irish seem to be of good stock," he chuckles. Nodding his head to emphasize his point, he continues, "Yes, he was a very good man. Had it not been for Father O'Connor, I wouldn't be here now. I wouldn't have had the opportunity to lead the life of joy and happiness I've been blessed with."

He looks again deep into my eyes and says, "I believe there is no better way on God's Earth to achieve happiness than to give comfort to those in need. When I first got to that small southern church, I was in bliss. In terms of land, we had a large parish, although few who lived there subscribe to our chosen faith." He smiles, and then chuckles again. "Those living in the South seem to take more comfort in being Baptists. Ah, well." He gives a slight wave of his hand. "God provides many routes into His Kingdom."

I begin wondering where this is going. I resist the temptation to look at my watch. I've always enjoyed Monsignor Ramón's way with a story. But right now, I'm thinking about Sandra. I don't want to be late on what might be a fateful date, wondering if this afternoon will be my first lunch with my future wife.

As if he sees my impatience, the Monsignor begins to move to the point. "After about a year, a young man joined our Church. He was just twenty-two and had come to town from someplace north and was looking for work. Later, when I looked back to that era of my life, I wondered what bad luck had brought him to our town. I've since written it off as fate. Or God's will." He again smiles his gentle smile. "Don't you think God's will and fate are one and the same?" He asks.

I hope when I reach an older age, I'll have this wise man's wisdom. He seems so able to understand the ways of God. He has done as he planned and has me anxious to see how God had tested him. My own faith is strengthened by my close proximity to my Monsignor.

"Jack." He looks at me to explain the newcomer's name. "His name was Jack. He did farming work and had not an ounce of fat on his hard body." Again the chuckle as he pats his own ample belly. "I was not quite as opulent then as I am now. But still, I wondered why Jack found me attractive." He looks me in the eye, and then nodding somewhat sadly, he says, "Please feel free to ask me what ever you want."

"What do you mean he found you attractive?" I ask.

"Weren't you his priest?" Although I've asked the question, I know where his story is leading.

Just because I've chosen to live a sheltered existence doesn't mean I'm naïve to the ways of the world. I've given confessions often enough to know that many men, and women too, are attracted to members of their own sex. I've listened to their admissions, and the terrible guilt attached. Such soul stripping shame has caused me to question the nature of sin. I've wondered about the difference between Original Sin and the man made variety, and wondered why loving another of one's own sex was a sin.

Why did an all-knowing and benevolent God create the forbidden fruit in Eden? Even before my recent disillusionment with God, my concern had been that it was man and not God that had invented the forbidden fruit concept. And many of the other sins that now plague man with guilt. I've often worried that man, through ignorance or greed, had made up a bunch of rules that a loving God would never consider. I think of the countless customs man has decreed as improper behavior at one time or another, and how the breaking of any of the many imposed rules imitates tasting the forbidden fruit.

In today's society, one of the forbidden lifestyles is an enduring love between members of the same sex. Many consider such a lifestyle horrific. The punishment for eating an apple in Eden has been mild throughout history, compared to what was in store for same-sex lovers.

My thoughts are blasphemously in conflict with the basics of my religion, but finding sin in two men being in love seems to stretch the meaning of sin. There's far too little love on Earth to start picking which is good love and which is sinful love. Having been so in love with Our Maker for these many years, I've come to recognize that love comes in all sizes and shapes. Many might find it strange that I've been in love with God. Thus, it's not for me to find fault in something as wonderful as love. Even to another man.

Chapter 16

Ramón's look beseeches me to understand what he's about to say. I smile as I return his look, realizing what a wonderful present he's giving me. He's not asking my forgiveness. He's only showing me that everyone's life, even his own, have crossroads. Everyone's life can take detours and run into barriers. It's the handling of the barriers and the final path taken that matters.

"Please continue," I beg. I wipe a bit of moisture from my eye. His story is touching my heart in ways I'd not expected. "I'll not interrupt again."

He shakes his head slowly. "Be sure you do interrupt whenever you feel like it. I want you to understand." With that said, he gets quickly to the point. "To make a long story short, I also became attracted to Jack. To say it took time and happened slowly is only a rationalization for what occurred. We became lovers."

He has not taken his eyes from mine. The courage of this man swells my heart. My mind jumps to how the hierarchy of our Church handled the situation. I ask, "Didn't the Church mind? It must have been noticed, even in a small parish in the South."

"I mentioned the presiding priest? Father O'Connor?" Again the serene smile from deep in his soul. "I guess I see a lot of him in you." He pats me lightly on the shoulder. "Our Church needs good men like him. And, good men like you."

I feel caught. He must have read my mind. He knows I'm going to bolt the priesthood and marry Sandra. How did he find out? Am I so transparent? I stammer, trying to get the words out, "Sir, I know I've been a disappointment these last few months.

But…." Should I lie and tell him I'm not thinking of leaving? My mind shuts down. My head drops

"There, there my son. I'm not telling my story to cause you discomfort. Of course I've noticed your wavering belief since you've come to my parish." He again smiles, looking at me. "Did you know I'd had my eye on you for a long time, even before we met? I saw the dedication in your work in Detroit, the type of dedication that comes from an endearing Love of our Lord. It could come from no where else."

I'm sadly shaking my head, as I mutter, "No, I didn't know you even knew I existed."

"I wanted a strong and loving man to watch over my parish when I'm gone. But, I realize something must have happened to you since then. Something seems to be different since you've come here. I don't know what, but I'm sure with the correct guidance, and a trust of our Lord, you will find your way. That's the reason I've wanted to tell you my story. I can only hope to be half the man that Father O'Connor was, but, with his guidance and our Lord's love, I'm here now."

I must be looking at him with surprise in my eyes. I had assumed he only wanted to let me know that he knew about my upcoming betrayal. Now I'm confused, but still curious. "Okay sir. I'm sorry I've again interrupted."

He pats my shoulder and then continues his story. "Of course Father O'Connor, found out about Jack and me. I'll never forget his attitude. He had a theory. He felt that about ninety-eight percent of mankind is good, decent and honest. That left about two percent whom he considered either the Satan or in close cahoots with Satan." Saying this actually brings a smile to both Ramón and me.

"Of course," he continues, "At any given time there seems to be another twenty or so percent that seem to be under the influence of those few true sinners. Father O'Connor felt I had become one of those unlucky twenty percent and was now being tempted by the Satan in the guise of Jack."

Is Monsignor Ramón saying Sandra is the Satan? He notices the look of shock on my face. His next words bring me some comfort. "Don't get me wrong, my son. There are few who truly live up to Father O'Connor's definition of evil." Again the comforting arm on my shoulder. "I doubt you would have any interest in pursuing such a person. Sadly, in my case, temptation led me to a truly bad person.

"Later, I came to realize that Father O'Connor was correct. Jack's entire interest in me was an attempt to tempt me away from The Church, an organization he somehow considered a threat to him. As I got to know Jack, I realized he felt anything that was good or decent was a threat to him personally. Jack was a somewhat twisted and wretched character. God rest his soul. I heard later that his life had become miserable, his body rotted with disease, and that he died an early death."

Monsignor Ramón then again chuckles, muting his last terrifying words. "I guess he didn't find my body attractive after all." He adds ominously, "Just my soul." He hesitates before saying, "Which he wanted to take with him to Hell. And he very nearly succeeded." He shakes his head sadly.

"There are very few henchmen of the devil, my boy. I'm not quite sure what you are thinking, but I know you need to put your trust in God and follow your heart. If you do that, I'm sure you'll come out of this just fine."

I feel compelled to confess my longing for Sandra. I began to talk, to tell him how I've sinned. As I begin to talk, he puts his hand up to stop me. "Let me continue my story, then we'll get you off to your lunch. If you feel the need to talk after that, I'll be here to listen." His eyes are again looking into the long ago past. "After my secret was discovered, I felt I must take off the collar and look for work elsewhere. But, Father O'Connor suggested I only take a leave of absence. He felt sure that if I took some time to reflect upon life and if I would continue with my enduring love of God, God would, as He does with all His children, bring me through that terrible time in my life."

"Did you go?" I ask. I've feared for days that Ramón will realize I've lost the faith and ask me to leave. I'm again thinking Monsignor Ramón's purpose is to ask me to resign. The fear again nagged at me as I began to worry that his story is only sugar coating and he will soon drop on me my worst nightmare. I'll have to leave the life I've loved for so many years. What will become of me? Panic overtakes me. In a matter of minutes, I've gone from an ecstatic high of fantasizing a life with Sandra, to a morbid low of no longer being a priest.

"Yes, I did go." He smiles up at me. "Not that I think you should take that drastic of a step." He smiles mischievously as he notices the look of relief as it crosses my face. He continues merrily, "I shan't allow you to leave until you get that back barn painted." He's referring to a shed on our church property I've been planning on turning into a teen club. "Even with that task done, the devil's going to have his own good time getting you away from me," He says with an elfish smile.

He then continues his story. "I can see now that I left the priesthood so I could think clearly. Father O'Connor also wanted me away from Jack and further temptation. I also noticed that, try as I might, my communication with God had ceased. I'd told my flock I was their voice to God, but God was no longer talking to me. I was living a lie."

What a surprise to find this wonderful little man had experienced many of the same impediments to Godliness that I've encountered the last few months. Although in my case, God not only has stopped talking to me, He has also ceased to exist. The only voice I hear now is the Devil's. Nevertheless, as I look at Monsignor Ramón, a slight hope begins to grow in my bosom. Maybe there is a God. Maybe He has only temporarily abandoned me and if I do the right thing I'll again have His love. "So, what did you do after you left The Church?" I ask.

His smile broadens across the full width of his face. "I joined the Peace Corp," he says.

My shock must have been apparent. Ramón actually starts to laugh. Deep belly laughs. He's enjoying this. "You did? I never knew that."

He's still rocking in laughter as he says, "This must be the feeling parents gets when they tell their children about their life before the first child was born. Yes, I did. I went to their regional office and told them I wanted the poorest, most miserable assignment they could find. I was going to punish myself for my sins. I'm surprised the Peace Corp didn't turn me down flat. They don't want martyrs. They aren't in the business of creating misery for atonement. What they need are dedicated people that actually want to help others. Had it not been for Father O'Connor, I'm sure I'd have failed in my quest for penance."

I smile at the thought of Ramón in the jungles of Africa. "So, you actually went?" I ask.

"Yep. After Father O'Connor talked to them, they took me at my word. I did the normal training after which they shipped me off to Brazil to a small village in the Amazon. I was given the nicest accommodations in the settlement and was treated by the people of the village like a king. But it was still a far cry from what I was used to. Although the meager food and sleeping on the floor somehow comforted me."

"The more my body suffered, the better my spirit felt. I worked hard during the days to help those destitute people learn ways to better survive. And with every night came my prayers to God. I never again broke my vowel of chastity even though I no longer had the obligation to lead a chaste life. Then one night God answered. A young woman was having a hard time of childbirth. Over the months of her pregnancy, I had come to respect her. She always had a bright smile and helping hand to give others. And now, here she was at the end of her pregnancy, suffering and about to die, as was her newborn. I asked God to take my life but save her and her child. I begged forgiveness for my sins."

Ramón has my rapt attention. Moisture again collects in the corners of my eyes. What a wonderful man I'm sitting next to. I can't say that his story has enabled me to suddenly love God again, but I do feel some hope. I say, "I take it he didn't take her life?"

"Nope. He spared both her and her babe. And my life as well. He's never again failed to answer when I've prayed. I knew in my heart He had forgiven me. I had atoned enough. As luck would have it, my tour of duty was over at the end of that month." Again, that deep smile as he looks up at me.

He gestures me to my feet, and follows me from the pew, saying, "My son, I don't think you've strayed as I had. It wasn't my heart I was following as I succumbed to Jack's temptation." He nods his head sadly, apparently thinking how he might have wasted his life. Then brightening, he looks directly at me, saying, "The lesson I'd like you to take from my little story is this. Follow your heart. If your heart leads you from the Church, I'll be the first to bid you a happy farewell. If Father O'Connor had not suggested I take a leave of absence, I'd not be here today to give you this fatherly advice."

We reach the door leading to the street. He pushes me along into the sunlight. "Go. Have a wonderful lunch. And always remember, God does indeed work in mysterious ways."

Chapter 17

I step through the door and into the daylight. Turning back, I give a tentative farewell wave to Monsignor Ramón. I thought my emotions could not be more buffeted than they've been thus far today. I find how wrong that assessment was as I walk away from the church and toward Sandra. I'm literally shaking in my boots. The symbolism of walking from a church I've loved wholeheartedly toward a woman I hope to love with equal strength is not lost on me. I square my shoulders and with resolve I head toward the street. I move steadily down the stairs toward the street. And toward Sandra.

As the Monsignor said, I've not strayed from the teaching of The Church as he had. Unlike Ramón's Jack, Sandra is a good and decent soul. Even my Monsignor will see that. I'd like to believe Ramón's point was to encourage me toward a married life. At least my heart, if not my soul, hopes that is what he was telling me to do.

My spirit begins to rise as I hurry toward my lunch date with Sandra. I step off the Church's property and onto the sidewalk. It couldn't have been lost on Sandra that I found her attractive. Her behavior toward me seemed to indicate the feeling was mutual. I cross the street and head toward the park where Jim and I had been jogging earlier today. My smile broadens as I replay in my mind my early morning conversation with Sandra.

Then my thinking takes a twist. I'm puzzled how my Monsignor had known about my difficulties and doubts I've had these last few months. What a coincidence. His telling me his story on the very day I'd resolved to change my life. I smile inwardly. If I were still a believer I'd certainly agree that God does work in mysterious ways. But, it's much easier to call it all a coincidence. All one big accident.

I follow the sidewalk that parallels the park toward the restaurant where I am to meet with Sandra. I focus on the flowerbeds that have been tilled for planting of petunias or pansies, or maybe even peonies. I'm feeling more light and silly and fanciful. I remember the garden I started in Detroit. It was a big plot of land, about one city block that had been donated to the church. Once the decaying buildings were torn down and the trash was removed, only the overgrown trees and shrubs were left. Knowing *"idle hands are the devil's tools,"* I had the idea of using the garden to keep busy the many mischievous hands of our parish. I touted the project as renovating the area into a natural landscape. Even though I knew there was precious little money that could be used for something as silly as a garden, somehow I knew God would provide. Despite my conviction, I was surprised by the support given my project. I had spun it as a natural landscape, hoping to save money by reusing what plants were already there. As long as it was touted as natural, we wouldn't have to spend precious money for fancy landscaping. Little did I realize that by calling it "natural" I'd given it a popular appeal. In hindsight, I realize that Middle America was on a binge to make everything "natural". My parishioners were hoping to emulate Middle America and thus find their way to that Promised Land.

It is funny what most people call "natural." When making a natural landscape, the first thing everyone wants to do is to clean up and remove all the dead logs and branches. It's as though God, if he had a choice, would naturally have his gardens cleared of all rotting material. People must think God has something against death and decay. Why is it no one recognizes that without decay there would be no nutrition to feed the next generation? And, without death God would have no friends and neighbors in Heaven.

A realization dawns on my. As in my past, once again I've been thinking of God and Heaven as though they exist. My thoughts have been the thoughts of a person who has a deep-seated belief in The Almighty. It's apparently a habit that is trying to survive. But, given how strongly I'd held my faith for all those years, it's no wonder I still think of God as a real and extant entity. I look around me somewhat embarrassed at having such silly thoughts in a town such as this, where material wealth far outweighs any spiritual wealth. And where decay is immediately cleaned up and death is kept well hidden.

When I was first approached to preside over this parish, I'd wondered how such an affluent area could possibly need soul saving. The community that is now surrounding me is a far cry from the poverty-ravished one I had worked with in Detroit. Upon making my decision to come here, I thought I'd realized something important. That being a priest in an affluent town might be a worthy calling. Saving the souls of the more able and well off people might be a workable solution to saving mankind. I'd thought then that maybe man's salvation lies in saving the souls of the most capable first. They in turn would begin the difficult task of saving the downtrodden.

As I look at the town around me, I realize my changed attitude requires a new outlook toward material wealth. These souls I find in this wealthy community do not need my help. Without a God there is no need to save souls. Much better to help the needy achieve the tools, which will enable them to live a better life. Much better to provide the poor with an education.

Since I seem determined to change my life drastically, I've begun to focus on the ramifications that I've been trying to ignore. I'll need to find work. Again I wonder what kind of work I'm fit for. The thought at first frightened me but now brings a smile to my face. I've not sought work since my summer jobs as a teenager, and even those jobs were just to mow lawns. Not quite the same as finding a way to support a wife and children. I certainly won't have to go to the extreme my Monsignor did. No Peace Corps in my future. Although, my reasons for leaving The Church will never be considered as socially inappropriate as Ramón's, I still think I will need to feel a sense of fulfillment in whatever profession I chose. Something fitting that will help mankind.

I'm well qualified to become a teacher. Even if I've never been a teacher in a formal sense, I've had the opportunity to teach.

In those poor neighborhoods of Detroit, I enjoyed the lessons I provided to those in my neighborhood. In Detroit, I loved the give and take of providing tidbits of knowledge to even the roughest guys on the block. Especially when I'd see the look of awe on their faces as the knowledge sunk in. There's not as much opportunity in this town to pass on my wisdom. Maybe I should teach in a poor parish for a parochial school. With the current shortage of teachers, many men have shed the cloth and instead of ministering, have taught for the church as a lay teacher, not as a priest.

There is no rule saying I have to believe in God in order to teach at a parochial school. There's only a requirement that I have the best of intentions for my students. A requirement that I will certainly fulfill. I need not broadcast my misgivings concerning God's existence. I don't have to tell the world about the voice that continually haunts me with doubts. It's not hypocrisy to teach the poor how to read and write even when I hear in my head that there is no God.

Having resolved how I might support my family and myself in my new life, I turn my thoughts elsewhere. I begin to imagine the upcoming luncheon with Sandra and how this lunch date might change my life forever. Then I remember Sandra's parting words that she'd be bringing a friend. I wonder who her friend is. I realize how little I actually know about this woman I'm resting my future on.

Does she have a boyfriend or is she only bringing a friend to approve of me as a date and future relationship? I don't even know where Sandra works or what she does for a profession. I'm determined to believe she's just bringing a girlfriend from work to meet me. Or possibly a sister or old college roommate. "She's probably just hoping for a friend's approval of me as a mate," I think to myself. That would be fine with me, since I can certainly understand wanting a friend's support.

I only hope I didn't misread her motive. I worry that I might not have heard her correctly. What if she is bringing her boyfriend with her? Maybe she's bringing the man she's planning to marry. Is it possible I'm such a neophyte in the ways of love that I hadn't even realized she's already attached? I begin to slow my pace as my mood again deteriorates.

I've always known I've had little experience with the emotional side of women. I know I have an ability to listen and interpret correctly whenever my parishioners would relate life problems. I've done this often with great success while acting as their counselor and confessor. But I have no experience with the inner workings of a woman's mind when her thoughts involve me. It's one thing to be able to see what's going on when a married couple comes to me for advice in their relationship. It's a whole different ball game when the mental gyrations have me as an object.

Remembering this morning's conversation with Sandra makes me surer of my self. I'm positive I can tell the difference between normal social intercourse and coquettish behavior. What went on between Sandra and me was not just social chitchat. Right up until the end, she was flirting. Making it plain that she thought of me as a worthwhile catch if I were only free of the priesthood. I can solve that. By mentally ripping my imaginary collar from my neck!

I look at my watch and realize I'm going to be a few minutes late. I lengthen my stride as I near the block where Sandra and her friend will be waiting. What irony that we'll be meeting at "Satan's Cathedral." I might be better off not having a God to believe in. Where once I would have worried about the wrath of God, I now find humor in rushing to a restaurant with such an irreverent name for a tryst with a woman.

I now have to force myself to think about Sandra and her friend. I see the restaurant at the end of the block. Although my nerves are getting more frazzled by the minute, I'm confident I'll see my way through the upcoming interview. How much more difficult could this be than weekly sermons? Those sermons where I'm trying to get people to live exemplary lives. I quickly close the distance between my meeting and me.

Entering the restaurant, I look around for Sandra. Having just come in from the bright sunshine outside, I have difficulty finding her due to the darkness inside the restaurant. I continue to scan the room, looking at each table. I finally see Sandra at a table along the back wall of the room. She's already seen me and is waving me over to join her and her friend. I'm taken aback. Her friend is not a sister or girlfriend.

As I approach the table, I see Sandra sitting with a man.

Chapter 18

My mood is mixed as I walk to the table. My spirits soar seeing Sandra again, even though she's dressed in work clothes rather than cute jogging shorts. Then I look at the man with her and begin to brood. He's a normal enough looking fellow, I suppose. Slightly shorter than me but with a full head of light brown hair and a friendly enough face. But why is he sitting here with my future wife? Having such a thought suddenly shocks me. What can I be thinking? A few weeks of preaching to this woman and one accidental meeting doesn't mean we will marry. Yet a feeling of fury overwhelms me.

Once before when I was a child, I had this same feeling. It was my first year trying out to be an alter boy. Everyone told me I was much too young to participate in this ritual. But I knew God would show me the way, and bless my wish. When the names of those selected were posted, my name was not there. Instead, a neighbor's name was on the list. I hadn't particularly liked the boy before that. After I saw his name, I absolutely detested him. That was the only time, until now, I'd felt hatred. I later learned that neighbor boy had made the list because he was two years older than I and also because the priest was trying to salvage a problem child. At the time though, rational thinking didn't alter my unfounded feeling of rage toward him, and the priest. The next year I actually did become an alter boy and the neighbor boy was asked to leave. Although my hatred toward the priest diminished, I became determined to make him realize his horrible error. I swore I'd be the best alter boy that priest would ever have. It took years before I resolved the strong negative emotions I had felt. I learned later in life to call the feeling jealousy. Could this feeling I now have, for the man sitting with Sandra, be jealousy?

I stand silently staring into the darkness for a moment in order to gather my wits. Both Sandra and the man she's with have cups of coffee in front of them. He sets his cup down as he sees me and, as I approach their table, he stands and reaches out his hand to shake. A sensation of paranoia overtakes me as I imagine that this man is only testing me, checking to see if I had failed to learn some important social etiquette in my cloistered life. But sanity regains a hold on my mind. After all, he is just offering to shake hands, I muse.

Somehow, I must overcome my unworthy feelings. I want Sandra to see me in my best light. I reach out and grasp his hand to shake. He says questioningly, "Hi. Father O'Malley? I'm Frank. Frank Johansen."

"Hi, Frank. Please call me Tommy," I respond. I'm sure he sees my plastic smile for what it is. I don't even know the man and already I hate him. What have I come to? What will become of me? I'm new to this jealousy thing. In fact, I'm new to all these feelings related to the opposite sex. The first time I had counseled a married man, he was working his way through a troubled time in his marriage. I was startled by his comment stating that love is hell. Until then, I'd only heard how heavenly love could be. Being a priest, I'd never been forced to truly examine this outlook on love. My Savior taught us to have love for all mankind. I only now realize how difficult it might be to love but one person, one woman.

I turn to Sandra. "Hi," I say. "How's your morning been?"

She smiles as she responds. "Actually, it started out wonderfully." Is she giving me a sexy flirting sort of smile or am I just imagining all sorts of things? I'm truly in over my head with these strange emotions. She continues, not knowing the turmoil she's putting me through. "Then my day got even better. And now I find myself sitting with two adorable men." She's smiling broadly as she looks first at Frank then me. I haven't a clue as to how I'm suppose to construe her comment, so I just sit down and shut my mouth.

She continues talking. "Since we got here a bit early, we've already ordered coffee. Let me get a waiter for you." She sees our waiter and waves him over. I sit next to Frank and across from Sandra. As I seat myself, I notice a large paperback book lying on the table. Since it's lying so it's open to some page, I assume they've been talking about the book.

The waiter stops and looks down at the three of us. He says, "May I take your orders now?"

Sandra takes the lead, looking quickly at each of us in turn. She must think she sees agreement on our face. Either that or she doesn't really care what we think. Her words set the tone of our lunch. "No. It'll be a while before we're ready to order lunch. But, perhaps Father O'Malley, uhhhh, Tommy, would like some coffee." At least she's going to treat me as a normal man by calling me Tommy. Spending an afternoon with her calling me Father O'Malley and thinking of me as a priest would be untenable.

Although I don't have much say over how our lunch is going to proceed, I can take control over what I drink. Since they are both having coffee, I'll have iced tea. In the recess of my mind, I recognize this childish attitude for what it is. Nevertheless, I look at the waiter and say, "No. Make mine an iced tea." I straighten my stooped shoulders and jut out my chin. There. I've taken charge.

The waiter leaves to fetch my drink. I again notice the book on the table. Its cover depicts a volcano spewing fire and ash. It reminds me of when I woke during the night. At that time, I'd felt as though a volcano was going off in my stomach, causing a horrible taste in my mouth. I hadn't thought about it then but now realize that the bitter lava coming up into my throat is what television commercials call acid reflux disease. I wonder briefly what people called it before the drug companies adopted such a scary name. An invented disease they use to sell more drugs so the companies can drug ever more people in the name of profit. Before the advertising men took charge, the disease was probably just known as a horrible taste in your mouth. In my case, I think that volcano that exploded in my gut, suddenly waking me, was prophetic of the day's events. Possibly even predicting the book lying on the table.

Indicating the book, I say, "I'm sorry if I've interrupted your conversation."

Frank responds, "Oh, that's fine. We were just talking about this book passed out in a seminar." Glancing between Sandra and me, he explains further. "I met Sandra at that seminar." He reaches for the book, inserts a bookmark at the page which had lain open, then closing the book he sets it next to his elbow. He then looks toward me and says, "Sandra has been telling me how you moved to our town only in the last year?" He makes the last comment a question.

I'm still feeling the lingering effects of the fury I felt when I first walked in and saw Frank with Sandra. But, I do have to admit, he certainly seems to be a pleasant chap. I might as well give him some of my history. As if he really cares all that much. It can't hurt. And, I reason, I still don't have to like him.

"Yes. I moved here from Detroit a few months ago. I'd been assigned to a parish in Detroit for about five years before that," I say. There. Now he knows all about me. In the recesses of my mind I still feel an uncomfortable angst. I'm not used to holding such anger toward a complete stranger.

Sandra speaks up. "He's being modest. Weeks ago I researched him and his Detroit church on the Internet. The neighborhood he was in is known to some as "Hell's Kitchen." I feel my face go hot with embarrassment. Sandra reaches over to pat my arm. As I stammer for something to say, the waiter saves me from further embarrassment. He arrives with my tea, which he sets in front of me. "Is there anything else for right now, or will you be ordering lunch later?" he asks.

Sandra quickly dismisses him by saying, "We'll order later."

I return to what she had just said about me. She cared enough about me to research me on the Internet? I had no idea she had any thoughts about me before today. It was true that many people, being so upset by the bleak conditions of the neighborhood where I lived in Detroit, named the area after the infamous "Hell's Kitchen" neighborhood in New York City. Some even contended that there was no neighborhood in America as bereft of wealth as those thirty square blocks I called home for my five years in Detroit. "I had no idea you knew where I'd been posted before we talked this morning." I stammer.

She first smiles at me, then turns to Frank, continuing to talk as though I'm not there. "Father O'Malley, I mean Tommy." She smiles at me as she honors my request to use my given name. "Tommy was written up often in the local newspapers for his work with the impoverished and downtrodden." She seems to warm up to her topic. She starts to talk about the garden I'd started and my project for opening a teen club. She even mentions my attempt at Big Brother and Big Sister affiliates in the neighborhood.

I feel my face taking on an ashen flaccidity. I don't care that Frank seems truly interested in the things Sandra is saying. I must stop all this talk. I'm here on an errand that is far from heroic. I will not let her make me into something I'm not.

"Thank you, Sandra, for caring enough about me to research my past. But that was all a long time ago." As I say this, I realize that in my mind at least this is true. It all seems to have happened in a different lifetime. So much has changed. Those tasks back in Detroit were easy. Every challenge was effortlessly met. I found all obstacles painless as long as I had God's love in my heart. No task seemed too daunting with the Almighty's power on my side. How different my feelings are now. Even the simple sermon I must write this afternoon seems beyond my abilities. I have no idea how I found the energy to deal with those hooligans in Detroit.

As my mind focuses on my many shortcomings, I hear Frank say how impressed he is. Looking at me, he says, "So, when did you decide you wanted to be a priest?" he asks.

This question has been asked of me many times. Until coming to my latest assignment, I've never had a problem answering the question with honesty. Saying I was in love with God was a useful way to begin a dialogue to help guide youngsters toward having an interest in The Church. Talking about God's love was a good way to extend a helping hand. But now, with my current intention to leave The Church, I fear that answering his question in my normal way will make me feel like a degraded hypocrite. Looking at Frank's earnest expression, I realize I won't escape his question.

"It all started actually before my tenth birthday," I tell him. When his eyes widen with curiosity and admiration, I feel I have to go on. I tell my story of being in love with God from a very young age, and knowing that I would do anything to work hand in hand with God to save suffering souls. I've been telling this same story for years, resulting in many different responses. There were those cynics who were far removed from anything other than the material world around them. Their attitude has always saddened me, knowing they had a long way to go before reaching the Kingdom of God. And then there were those who seemed to admire what I did, as though I were the god. They never seemed to understand what I was saying. They never realized it was because of God's love that my life had become blissful. It certainly wasn't some attribute of mine. It was a miracle given to me by another. By God.

Chapter 19

Sandra saves me from further embarrassment by grabbing the menus we'd set aside and handing them out to Frank and me. "I'm starving. Let's order," she says. Just like that, I've been given a moment to evaluate how Frank is receiving my story. I notice that there's something unusual in Frank's as he listens to what I've been telling him. Most people don't actually listen when another person is talking. Rather, they are only using that time to figure out what they themselves are soon going to say. That's obviously not true of the man in front of me. An eerie feeling starts to overtake me. I'm being confronted by a different sort of fellow than I usually meet. Frank truly understands what I'm talking about. It shows in his eyes. He's not projecting his own preconceived idea into my story. I'm being encouraged to continue telling my tale and am eager to do so. I've never before had someone so fully understand what I'm saying.

The waiter notices us looking at our menus and comes over to take our order. "Have you decided what you'd like for lunch?" he asks.

As is customary in our culture, we all look to Sandra to give her order first. She says, "Yeah. I'd like the Chef's Salad. No dressing." She smiles at Frank and me as we shake our heads. "Okay, okay. I watch what I eat. Besides, greasy fat food is for men."

As if he needs to prove her point, when asked for his order, Frank says, "I'd like the large bacon cheeseburger with fries." He nods his head for emphasis, as he smiles at Sandra and gives a quick wink toward me.

It's as though I'm entering a male conspiracy. I enjoy the feeling of a budding friendship. When the waiter turns to me, I say, "I'll have the same." Then I make clear who my fellow conspirator is. "The burger. Certainly not what she's having."

We all chuckle as the waiter leaves with our order. A moment later, our waiter comes back with a pot of coffee in one hand and pitcher of iced tea in the other. We sit silently as he fills first the coffee cups, then my glass.

When we are again alone, I look toward Frank. "Frank, what do you do for a living? Are you a psychologist or psychiatrist or something like that?" I assume this from his uncanny ability to understand what I'd told him about my past. As an undergraduate in college and also at the seminary, I took a number of psychology classes in order to prepare myself for the counseling I knew I'd be doing. It was in those psychology courses I first realized what counselors are actually doing while their patients are talking. They listen, but only for those tidbits that will prove a point that they've already decided on. Once the patient has seemed to say what is expected, the shrink can then tell their patient some made up method they hope will handle the problem. I soon realized that actual understanding is not a prerequisite for psychological counseling. Instead, telling the patient what to do and how they'd better interpret their thoughts and respond, is foremost to a psychologist or psychiatrist. What's laughingly called the "mental health" industry seems insistent on telling people a preconceived notion of how they should live their lives. Sadly funny from an industry that has such a high suicide rate.

When I first started counseling as a priest, whenever I tried telling someone what to think, my parishioner would get mad. Either that, or he would lose all hope. I decided to try something new. So, I listened, and would truly try to understand what my parishioner was saying. Even though I didn't always agree with what the person would tell me, I'd still endeavor to understand his position. I learned I could never tell people they had to love God, or have faith. I could only show the way. I found out the hard way that evaluating is a bad substitute for understanding.

I envy Frank's ability to listen. If he' is trained as a psychologist, I'll have to rethink my opinion of the profession. His response to my question is a surprise. His smile quickly turns to a good-hearted chuckle. "My goodness no!" He exclaims. "I hope you think better of me than that." Observing my confusion, he continues, "I do give seminars, though. I'm teaching a new type of counseling. It uses a technique so foreign to psychology, I'm afraid they often frown at it. A form of counseling allowing the person himself to determine what's right or wrong."

This man is quickly endearing himself to me. How can his thoughts concerning psychology so closely parallel my own? I ask, "So, you give seminars as a living?"

His answer once again shocks me. "Actually only in the evenings and on the weekends." He smiles. "I'm a chiropractor and have an office just east of here. So, evenings and weekends are when I do the seminars. I also do some one-on-one counseling. We use a new technique described in this book." He indicates the book he and Sandra had been looking at when I came in.

My utter confusion must be apparent to both Sandra and Frank. Sandra joins in the conversation. "It was at one of his seminars where I met Frank." She smiles at him as she continues. "Actually, I was lucky enough to have Frank show me the counseling technique first hand. He took me on as a demonstration. At the time, I thought he had a screw loose and would humiliate us all. But that half hour session changed my life."

Again I feel that flittering of jealousy and rage kicking in. I don't want to hear that this guy is impressive. In fact, I would far prefer if he weren't. Just this morning, Sandra was giving me these same looks of admiration. I don't want her to be giving this kind of appreciation to another man.

I realize I have much to learn if I'm going to be leaving the protection of the Church and enter the lay world. I have a newfound respect for all those men who have had to deal with the devils of jealousy and lust. I'm learning the consequences of obsessing over a woman's mind, body and soul.

A priest never gets to enjoy matrimony. Although we celebrate seven sacraments, including the sacrament of matrimony, we ourselves never marry. An oversight by the founders of our church, I'm sure. Although the current hierarchy in The Church spins it to sound as though we priests rise above marriage. In my less cynical days a mere year ago, I would have said I had no need for the wonders of marriage. I was in love with God and married to His Church. What a difference a year makes. For the first time in my life I begin to think about the rewards inherent in a beautiful body such as Sandra's. But just because I want to enjoy the beauty of a rose doesn't mean my blood must boil in lust and jealousy. With difficulty I control my resentment of Frank. After all, Sandra is only saying she respects what this man did for her in a seminar. When I look at it in that way my curiosity returns. "So are you wanting to sell me a seminar?" I ask. I'm being slightly serious and somewhat sarcastic. Being a priest doesn't mean I've had no experience with con artists.

Frank again puts me off balance. With a smile wrapped around a serious demeanor he says, "No, although I do sell the seminars." He chuckles. "I can't seem to get anyone to give me free office space or free help. He says in mock exasperation as his hands go up in the air. "So I do have to charge to cover the costs. But, in your case, I feel differently. When Sandra came to me this morning and told me about you and your history of good works, I was impressed."

Again I'm embarrassed. Glancing at Sandra, I quietly murmur, "Thank you. That's very nice." Sandra's hand reaches over to pat mine. I'm quickly being conditioned to compliment this woman. It's how Pavlov's dog must have felt. Whenever he reacted correctly, he too got a reward. Each time I compliment Sandra, she reaches over and pats my arm. I worry I'll be drooling just as Pavlov's dog did. With luck, I might get very accustom to Sandra's heart felt touches.

As she leaves her hand touching my own hand, she says, "The idea hit me as we were jogging this morning, when you told me about your loss." Her eyes are focused intensely into mine.

Chapter 20

A higher being than me must be controlling my life. What Sandra has just said has me in a fit of confusion. I need a moment to ponder Sandra's comment. As luck would have it at that precise moment, our food arrives. A miraculous moment allowing me to collect my thoughts. As the waiter sets his tray on a side table I hear Frank and Sandra saying those inconsequential things people often say as their food appears.

Frank's voice booms, "Thank God, I'm famished."

Sandra teasingly says to the waiter, "The gross red meat goes to the barbaric men. Yummy, that salad looks delicious."

I sit silently. Our food is passed to each of us. In a daze, I take my plate from the waiter. The respite from our previous conversation allows me time to untangle what's been said. But I'm confused. What loss? What's Sandra talking about? I know I told her I had feelings for her. I'm sure I made that clear. I'm also sure I made it clear that I will be vacating my position at the Church at which time I'd be honored to see her on a social basis—a man-to-woman basis.

Had Sandra taken my comments as an insult? What I took as preliminary courting, she might have found humiliating? Worst yet, degrading? But why would she consider my interest in her degrading? I realize I'm no movie star. But I've never thought of myself as degraded? The confusion from my feelings toward Sandra has me reeling. At this point, I'm certain that wooing a woman is far beyond my meager abilities.

Not realizing what horrible scenarios I'm visualizing, Frank and Sandra continue their good-humored banter about the pros and cons of red meat over salads. I woodenly chew away at my hamburger. If they notice my silence, they make no mention.

In years past, the men in my parish would often joke with me about their women, telling me how lucky I am that I don't have to unravel that impenetrable knot called a woman's mind. Almost every married man I've talked to about this would tell me that if a husband can't read a woman's mind, both day and night, then he's going to be in mighty big trouble. They said this half in jest as they looked furtively out of the corner of their eye, making sure no women was eavesdropping. Despite their strong statements to the contrary, these men would add that they'd have it no other way. The wonders of womanhood were well worth any sacrifice.

For the first time in my life I feel a kinship with those married men. I'm certainly not able to read Sandra's mind. I obviously haven't a clue what she means when she refers to my loss. What loss have I endured? My eating slows as my dazed look becomes more obvious.

Sandra apparently sees my pain. "Father O'Malley" she begins. I start to interrupt with a complaint about her use of my title. A title I certainly don't feel I deserve. She holds up her hand to stop me. "Please let me continue." She looks at me beseechingly. "I must tell you my thoughts. And my feelings."

Apparently the personal nature of what is coming dawns on Frank. With little ado, he sets his hamburger onto his plate, stands up and says, "Excuse me. I think I need to go to the bathroom." Then he turns and walks off.

Again Sandra starts, her hand still firmly planted on mine. "Father O'Malley. I have to tell you something wonderful, but difficult, that happened to me this morning." Her eyes actually are shining from unshed tears.

I'm enthralled but fearful of what I'm going to hear. "Okay. I'll stay silent," I say although I want to stop her from continuing. I want only to profess my love for her. To tell her how I will cherish and protect her. Instead, I say, "Please continue."

She begins to smile as she says, "This morning, a very sexy and gorgeous man was flirting with me." Her tear filled eyes turn to mischief in an instant. The impenetrable knot called a woman's mind is again evident. She's teasing me now. Although, given her preamble, I fear what will follow.

"Even more than that, I started to imagine what a great life I could have with such a man." Her hand on mine squeezes lightly. I'm on the verge of tears myself. Whether from overwhelming relief or overwhelming sadness, I can't tell. She continues, this time using my preferred given name. "Tommy. You are a wonderful, and beautiful man. And as I said, very sexy. Any woman would do almost anything to be with you." She smiles sexually, then wickedly. "I mean that. In a very biblical way." She winks. Could she be leering?

She gives one last pat to my hand then she deliberately moves her hand to her side of the table. I'm afraid my unshed tears will soon become tears of anguish. I'm not enjoying this conversation in the least. I promised this woman I'd keep quiet to let her have her say. I vow to do so as I continue to sit stoically.

"As I mentioned to you a few minutes ago, an idea came to me when you said you'd lost your love for God. I realized then that if I could, I'd help you with that pain. Even if it meant losing you as a man."

In a million years, with the insight of a million men, I would never have predicted this reaction from Sandra. My saying I'd been in love with God somehow effected her? How could such an abstraction make such an impression? I'm embarrassed and humiliated. Maybe she's having her fun at my expense. Doesn't she realize that God is only a figment of our imagination? That I'd only been in love with an idea? There is no God. Those words keep rolling through my mind. I decide to ignore her statement. I'll assume she's only showing a slightly cruel sense of humor. No one's perfect.

Whatever her motivation, Sandra is not acting as though she's joking. Or being cruel. She's acting very somber about something. The beautiful young woman in front of me looks very serious. Very serious indeed. She's leaning far across the table toward me. Her arms spread in front of her. It's as though she's trying to reach into my mind and convince me of something.

"I don't know if you knew, but a few months ago, my father died." She says this as though she's decided to change the subject.

I inwardly sigh from relief. I didn't like thinking Sandra was capable of making fun of me or being cruel at my expense. Now I see she had only mentioned my disenchantment with God as a way to bring our conversation around to her, and what is a much greater trauma. The death of her dad. Whenever I hear about the death of a person's loved one, I also feel their grief. Being empathetic is often a curse. The pain I feel for Sandra is real, even though it's only vicarious.

"I'm sorry," I say. I mean it, despite the fact that Sandra isn't acting as though she's grieving. I'm sure she's not so coldhearted that she'd joke about her own father's death. I'm confused about her matter of fact attitude. In order to understand her behavior I ask "Were you close?"

Sandra pulls herself back to her side of the table and picking up her fork begins to dawdle with her salad. Watching her thinking things through, or even playing with her food is a delight. Even though I'm romantically enticed by her, I can be enough of a friend to put those thoughts aside and listen to her sad story. As the silence drags on, I wait patiently for her to speak.

"Very close," she finally says. "I was absolutely devastated. For weeks, I could hardly get out of bed."

Of course I believe her. She has no reason to lie about such a thing, although she doesn't look to be a woman recently devastated. As I ponder her comment I nibble at the last of my French fries. Looking at her now, she certainly seems lively for someone who had been so depressed she couldn't get out of bed. How am I to explain her sprightly demeanor? People who have experienced a devastating event carry the effects with them for years. Some people never get over the loss of a loved one. Where had her depression gone? Despite my lingering doubts about her seriousness, my training to comfort the bereaved kicks in. Reaching over to pat her hand I say, "I'm sure your father knew you loved him. I'm sure he left this world a happy man, having you for a daughter. I have no doubt that he's now looking down at you with pride." Even with my shaken faith, such words come easily. It's what years of training and practice will do.

Sandra smiles pleasantly. She says, "Thank you, Father." Despite her acknowledgment of my reassuring words, she's not acting as though I've had any effect on her. Her next statement explains why. "If it hadn't have been for Frank and his seminar I think I'd have just died." She points to Frank who is just now returning from the back hallway. He looks questioningly toward our table, so Sandra waves him over to join us again. She pushes away her empty salad plate, wipes her mouth with her napkin, and tosses it onto the table. Then, leaning back into her chair, she smiles as she continues. "Without what Frank did, you certainly wouldn't have had me to jog with this morning. Or if I had been able to get to the park, you wouldn't have found me at all attractive." She's flirting and teasing once again.

Again, her mentioning how Frank has impacted her life. I realize it's not my words of comfort or some sermon I'd given that brought Sandra back from the brink. It was something about that strange technique Frank teaches. As I ponder this guy that's been such a puzzle for the last hour, he approaches our table. As he reaches our side, Sandra looks up at him and says, "I just told Father O'Malley about my loss, and how you helped me." Frank sits down, looks at me, and nods with understanding.

Chapter 21

My bewilderment must be apparent. Given Sandra's words and the look on her face, she must feel she's said something significant. Frank seems fully cognizant of her thoughts. It's only me that's missing something. A piece of some puzzle. I'm still somewhat in a daze concerning Sandra's and my private conversation. She started out saying I was sexy and a great catch. I'm sure she said something like that. Then she started talking about her dad dieing. And then Frank came back to the table. I think I'll become a monk even though I no longer believe in God. That would be far less confusing than trying to keep up with the mechanics of a woman's mind.

Frank comes to my rescue. He says, "Tommy. Sandra came to me this morning and asked if I was interested in helping you with a similar situation." Seeing my confusion, he adds, "When I helped her concerning her dad's death."

Part of the puzzle becomes clear. When Sandra had told me how devastated she'd been when her dad died she was describing feelings she no longer had. That's why she wasn't acting as distraught as my parishioners would in the same situation. My experience is that after having lost a loved one, people go through the psychological cycle from denial to acceptance. The cycle takes years. Since Sandra's dad had died only months ago, she should have still been experiencing considerable sorrow. But I just don't see in Sandra any ill effects of a recent and difficult loss. Only a healthy sadness over a recently departed father. Apparently Frank had helped her overcome any debilitating grief.

I'm still puzzled by their insistence on comparing Sandra's state of affairs to a situation they seem to think I've had. My parents are both in fine health. Granted, I haven't been to see them in some time. But I hear from both my siblings often and they tell me my folks are having the time of their lives in retirement. My sister Maggie even said that the occasional fights they would have when we were children are gone. In the place of the acrimony is an almost giddy love. Apparently the stress and strain of earning enough money to send three children to college took its toll. The pressure on my parents would often erupt into domestic fights. Once we three kids were living our own lives, the pressure on my parents went away. In its place came a golden older age. Whenever my sister mentions how much better they are now doing, I feel a twinge of guilt that my educational expenses added to their earlier anxiety.

Since my parents are fine, what is it Frank and Sandra keep referring to? I tackle this confusion head on. "Why do you keep talking about my loss?" I ask. "As a kid, both my grandparents on my father's side died and I did take that hard. But it's been decades and I've come to accept it as...." I stammer for a moment. I was going to say, "As the will of God." But then I realize that God is gone from my life. I continue, "I've accepted death as inevitable. I never knew my other grandparents, and my parents are both doing just fine."

Frank and Sandra give each other knowing looks, as though they've noticed I'd neglected giving God credit for death. They begin to talk at the same time. They both seem to have something to say that will answer my questions. They chuckle easily together, reminding me of my earlier jealousy. They're far too comfortable in each other's presence. If it weren't for my own interest in this woman, I'd be happy seeing two people so at ease. As it is though, my jealously is too close to the surface.

Frank finishes his hamburger with a relish and stacks his plate on top of Sandra's. He transfers all the utensils to my empty plate, places my plate on top, and pushes the used dishes to the far side of the table. Obviously, a very organized man.

Sandra must agree with my assessment of Frank. She hands him the reins of the conversation. "Go ahead, Frank. You're certainly the expert here." She smiles and chuckles lightly.

Frank looks directly at me. Again that interested look. Not really an intense stare, just a look as though he really cares. When I first started dealing with parishioners one-on-one I'd practice that sincere and caring attitude while looking in a mirror. I knew a professional must look the part. A priest must care, so I practiced a caring demeanor. I finally gave it up. Looking in the mirror for verification of my concern was missing the point. Instead, I just started to listen to what I was being told and I actually began to care for the person. After that the demeanor just magically appeared. Pretending is a bad substitute for understanding. I pull my attention back to Frank.

"Tommy," he starts. "Sandra told me about your conversation concerning your love for God. If I've understood correctly, it was that love that led you into priesthood. And that love which has kept you steadfast, up until recently when you lost it. Tommy, that's what we keep talking about. Your loss of God's love."

I shake my head in disgust. I start to get up, then sit back down, deciding that I must clear up a misconception. For God's sake! These two people don't know the difference between the love of an illusion and the loss of one's own father! My God Almighty! How can they think these are the same? I shake my head in protest.

Frank continues, "I can see how you might not think the death of a parent is the same as losing a heartfelt love. Can you give me a moment to explain?" He hesitates as he awaits my permission. Summoning the will to remain open minded I nod for him to continue.

"It has to do with the technique I've had such success with." He indicates the book lying on the table between us. I try to control my unease. I'm sure these two people have the best of intentions. I doubt they are only pulling some cruel hoax. Neither one of them are laughing. They act as though it's not a silly notion of mine that I'd had God's love, and now I'm grieving over its absence. All they're doing is taking me at my word. Why is it that

I feel I must make light of my misfortune, and make it complicated?

"Okay," I say. "But, I just don't see how the two compare."

Frank begins to talk, but not about loss. He tells me about his early days when he was just learning his new technique. He says, "I learned early on it's not what I happen to feel that should be causing a person's pain. When I first began, I thought I knew what people should be thinking and what would be the solution to their problems." He smiles slightly wistfully. " But, with experience, I learned something entirely different. It was not what I thought was causing a person's pain that mattered. What I so arrogantly felt was the source of their problem was usually not correct." Frank sadly shakes his head. "This arrogance is what gets the psychiatrists and psychologists into trouble. Arrogance, and of course, those stupid drugs they insist on giving everyone."

With his last statement, I begin to take Frank seriously. Working in Detroit had shown me the devastation drugs do. Even prescribed drugs usually caused more harm than good. How in the world can an industry that professes to help mankind believe that drugging people is going to somehow help? He's gotten my interest. "What do you mean?" I ask. "Although I agree with you that drugging everyone makes the job of getting people off drugs much harder. But what does that have to do with whether you know the answer to a person's problems?"

Frank nods his head in understanding. "I'll admit I've only done a cursory study of the field of the old-fashion mental health industry, although, I've certainly talked with a number of people that have been victims of psychiatry or psychology. One for one, I've been told that the standard in the industry is to learn a bit about a person, then proceed to tell him what the self-proclaimed experts thinks he should do about it." Frank smiles a sad smile. After a moment, his smile brightens and he says, "Getting back to what we've been talking about, I think only the person himself can possibly know what ails him. That's the genius of what I've been practicing and teaching these many years. It's what you think you lost, not what Sandra or I might think. It's an opportunity for you to discover what is true for you."

Just this morning, while jogging with Sandra, I'd been thinking about this very subject, and realized I had helped others the most when I let them decide for themselves the answers to their questions. My affinity toward Frank continues to grow. I just wish he didn't look quite so comfortable sitting next to Sandra.

Sandra speaks up. "I can give you a little first hand experience. As I've told you, I was more than devastated when my father died. Looking at it now, I realize I wasn't going through a normal grieving period."

How can she say she'd been so hurt when she's acting this healthy in such a short time? Maybe I'm still granting too much credit to people that claim to be mental health experts. It's far too easy to just accept those people's definition of normal, and to believe them when they insist that if we don't conform to their ranting, then we are the abnormal ones. Maybe, I should just open my mind and listen to another person's viewpoint.

"When Frank offered to see if he could help me find the source of my grief, I of course thought he was nuts." With this, she smiles and pats his arm. I realize she's only trying to soften words that Frank might take as an insult. I only wish she'd find a way rather than touching him. Apparently my jealousy is going to remain unabated. Despite my frown, she continues with what she's saying. "On the surface, it seemed obvious to me what caused my pain. My father had just died. This didn't seem to be rocket science to me." Again she smiles toward Frank, "Actually, Frank had a session with me that day and then again the next day."

My head turns between Frank and Sandra with confusion. "What do you mean he had a session with you?" My jealousy now has me worrying about the sexual antics psychiatrists call therapy and I want no part of anything like that.

Sandra's next words calm my fears. "I guess a session would be considered a form of talk therapy. Very similar to how you work one-on-one with your parishioners. For me, it was an invitation to look into my past and discover my own truth. It was on the second day that I started to look at my earliest memories of my father." She smiles a sweet smile as the pleasant memories engulf her. Then she takes on a serious demeanor as she continues, "If it hadn't been for Franks ability to get me to remember long forgotten memories I'd never have been able to revive those wonderful days. My father had become my knight in shining armor, straight from the fairy tales he read to me every night. It was during that time that I'd decided all of my happiness in life would depend on my daddy." She chuckles as she realizes her voice has taken on the tone of a little girl. It's clear that Sandra has no doubt it was Frank that provided this miracle.

As she continues to tell her story of self-discovery, I wonder if life can be so simple. Might my sudden dismissive nature toward God be rooted in my childhood memories? If so, why don't I just remember the offending times and right my own life? Why would I need another to guide me? This thought brings me back to Frank. What's in it for him?

Sandra is looking at me with a sweet angelic smile. She again reaches out to affectionately touch Frank's arm. "Who would have thought that a simple decision when I was a kid would have made me so sad at this age? I knew my dad was my idol, but to depend on him for all of my happiness was pretty silly." Sandra looks at Frank and says sincerely, " I really do want to thank you. Again."

She turns toward me. "Tommy, I can't say that what happened to me will happen to you." I again detect that mischievous sexy smile on her face as she continues. "And, if after you look at all the options you still think we should see each other, well, I'm sure somewhere in that big old church of your is my phone number." With that, she looks at her watch and says, "Well guys, I'm late. Unlike you two, I neither work for myself, nor God. I have a taskmaster as a boss."

She starts to pull her wallet from her purse. Both Frank and I realize together that this independent woman is planning on paying for lunch. I first get my words out. "Both of you are trying to do me a favor." I smile as I add, "It's yet to be seen if it's ill advised. Nevertheless, let me pay for this lunch for all of us. Just the opportunity to see a different slant on what's going on with me is worth far more than the cost of our lunches."

My words have their intended impact. Frank nods his head and says, "Fair enough."

Sandra puts her purse back together and leans over to give me a small kiss on the cheek. As she pulls away, she says, "Better than trying to find my phone number, why don't we meet later today. I'm planning on having an after work drink right here in the bar at six o'clock this afternoon." As she says this, I recognize another change that has occurred to me on this strange day. A beautiful woman is asking me to share a social drink with her. I'm being asked out on a date. I'm going to have to tell my friend Jim we won't be able to meet as we had planned. I'm sure he will understand why I would rather be on a date with Sandra. She continues, "I really hope you'll have a drink with me. And you can tell me how things go when you're with Frank this afternoon." She smiles broadly at both of us. She leaves us with her parting words, "And don't bring Frank with you."

With that, she turns toward the door and sashays away.

Chapter 22

"What was that all about?" I ask. I'm shocked by what I take as Sandra's rudeness to Frank. I've gone from being jealous of her feelings toward Frank to being appalled that she would so simply throw him aside. Frank saves me from my conflicting emotions. With a good-hearted chuckle he says, "She's quite a gal. I think if you weren't in the priesthood, you wouldn't stand a chance of avoiding her womanly wiles."

When I again try to object to how he'd been dismissed, Frank informs me of his ongoing relationship with a woman he's known for a couple years. "In fact, its Sandra that has kept me from losing my girlfriend." He hesitates for a moment and then continues. "My girlfriend's name is Patty. Sandra made it clear that if I didn't want to lose Patty, I'd better get on the stick and ask her to marry me." I see a human side to this man that had been missing earlier. He's actually looking slightly chagrin like a cat that has been caught eating a canary.

"You see Sandra and I have become the best of friends. She's like the sister I never had," he says wistfully.

"That's nice to hear. I had no idea what your relationship was with Sandra," I say. Once again I see how difficult and confusing the world has become now that it contains relationships with the opposite sex. I begin to realize the wisdom in keeping priest's celibate. A practice that both serves God and helps maintain a priest's sanity. Although priests never go through the difficult process of learning how to deal effectively with women, celibacy also results in priests missing many of the nuances life holds for lay people.

Frank chuckles, and then says jokingly, "It's refreshing to see a confident man stagger under the perplexing spell cast by a woman. I thought it was only me who turned into a mass of jelly when I'm near the one I adore."

I've had very few close friendships with a man. Perhaps it's a lacking in my personality. Maybe I've kept myself too aloof from those souls I felt were in my care. Now, though, a friendship seems to be growing between Frank and me. What an unexpected pleasure. Before my emotions completely choke me up, I change the subject "If I understand correctly what Sandra has been saying, she thinks my recent renunciation of The Church is not very severe, and that it's only a temporary aberration that I'll soon overcome when I come to my senses."

Frank nods in agreement. "Yep. I think she does see it that way. Don't get her wrong. Sandra's a very smart lady." In case Frank agrees with Sandra's conclusion, I begin to protest, believing in my heart that my recent feelings concerning God and The Church are grounded in logic.

Frank continues, ignoring my interruption. "I think utmost in her mind is saving your soul." He continues with a barrage on my recent reluctance to stay in The Church. "Think of it from her point of view. She's been smitten by you." He arches his eyebrow, questioning whether I'll disagree with what he'd just said. "She's smart enough to realize that she'd never have the happiness she feels she deserves if, in your heart, you feel you're doing the wrong thing. She recognizes that taking you from a church you might again come to trust, would be condemning you both to a life of hell." His brooding vision makes me wonder if fire and brimstone could be preferable to a living with me being depressed.

Self-analysis has never my strength, but I'm afraid what Frank and presumably Sandra think about my depression could come true, given how my mood has swung today.

He pauses for a moment, he then continues, "Since Sandra first told me about you, I had hoped I might be able to do something to help. Now having had an opportunity to get to know you, it's apparent you're a good man who has done many admirable things. But it's mostly for Sandra I'm offering my help.

A little present I want to give to my adopted younger sister." He smiles again.

"Thank you," I mummer. I'm not sure if I'm thanking him for his compliment to me or his willingness to give something to the girl I adore. I recognize though, I'm slowly being led toward an unknown. I'm becoming convinced to try something new and different. Although I don't understand this technique Frank keeps referring to, I trust Sandra when she said her sessions with him had changed her life.

In the recesses of my mind I again hear the words Ramón said to me earlier today. God works in mysterious ways. I'm being presented with one of God's mysteries. It looks as though I might be forced to face one of life's mysteries, whether or not God exists. If I still had my faith, I might be more curious than fearful, embarking on what might be one of God's mysteries adventures.

More rationally, I think of a future with Sandra. If both Frank and Sandra believe these meetings might help, I have nothing to lose, and quite possibly a woman's heart to win. "Okay. What is it you want from me?" I ask.

The waiter comes over to clear our table. As the dishes are being removed, Frank looks at his watch, and says, "It's almost one-thirty. We've probably tied up this table long enough with our chit-chat." He waves around at the still crowded restaurant we've been in for the last hour and a half. "You offered to buy lunch. I thank you." He says with a chuckle and nod of his head. "I have a quiet place about a half mile from here. It's where I give seminars and do some of the counseling I've mentioned. I need to visit the restroom, so how about my meeting you outside? I imagine you walked here from your church so, if you want, we can use my car and continue our discussion over at my storefront."

I nod my agreement as he gets up. My eyes follow him as he retreats toward the back of the restaurant. What am I getting myself into? I again notice the book he and Sandra had been discussing when I arrived. The words Dianetics, and apparently the author, L. Ron Hubbard, are splashed across the cover. I pick it up to see what I can determine about my upcoming adventure. I've never heard of the book or the author. A consequence of living a cloistered life I suppose. Many current crazes pass me by without my knowledge.

I twist and turn the book in my hands as though the knowledge held within will transfer to me by osmosis. If the size of a book proves its worth, this book should be very valuable. Over five hundred pages. The index alone is ten pages long. I thumb through the book and then read the first few lines of the synopsis. Comparing the discovery to fire might be hyperbole, but then again, there have been discoveries by men that are miraculous. Again I look at the front cover and worry that I haven't a clue as to whatever adventure this book and Frank have to offer. But if it's the way to Sandra's heart, then so be it.

Frank reenters the main dining room. I hastily pull out my billfold and place sufficient bills on the table to cover our lunch and a tip. I pick up the book and then say to Frank as he approaches, "I assume you want to take the book with us?"

"Yeah. In fact, I have a number of those. Why don't you take that one as a gift? Maybe when you have time later you can take a look at it. Tell me your thoughts. From a Catholic priest's point of view."

We exit the restaurant and head toward his car, which is parked across the street. I begin to feel edgy as I crawl into the front seat. As silly as it might seem, I've been forcing myself to be courageous to prove to Sandra that I will be an understanding, yet strong and suitable mate. I pray my many years of priesthood haven't closed my mind in such a way that I can't try something new. Yet, despite this new feeling of love, and what now seems to be a hypocritical prayer, I'm apprehensive as I anxiously await whatever it is that Frank has in mind for me. I have often looked at books that have touted the newest fad in psychological babble. Although most fads contain a bit of useful common sense, my experience has shown that even common sense, when mixed with a bunch of idiotic theories, can be worst than useless. Grim thoughts about the Antichrist give me a feeling of foreboding.

I ask Frank, "I've never heard of this guy or this book. Is it new?"

As we continue driving toward his office, Frank gives me a quick summary on the books history. "The research for the technique was done decades ago," Frank answered. "But then the author ended up spending all his time lecturing about it rather than doing it, so he decided to write the book explaining the theory and process. It became an instant best seller." He looks over at me as he continues. "Since that time, the procedures have been used successfully throughout the world."

Although Frank seems too polite to mention my never having heard about a best seller, I hope he doesn't think I'm unread and unschooled. I hope he realizes that my secluded life as a priest explains why I've not come into contact with the book.

We pull into a parking space next to an attractive building. There is an imprinted name within the awning proclaiming this office as a Life Improvement Center. That must be a positive message for many. I'm sure I'm not the only one needing an improved life.

Frank gets out of the car and leads me into the building. He unlocks the door leading to a front office. "Come on in. I'll show you around." As we walk down the hallway, he points out his reception area and some books he has for sale. The titles I see seem to have been written by the same person. This L. Ron Hubbard certainly seems to be a prolific writer.

Frank shows me the area where his seminars are held, a room with many chairs facing a podium on a slightly raised stage. Walking toward the back of the suite, he shows me into his office. "This is where I do the one-on-one counseling. Go ahead, make yourself comfortable." He says indicating a small couch along the wall.

Ignoring the couch, I sit down in a chair across from the couch. Frank explains how we'd be identifying and talking about various incidents in my past. My concern that he is going to hypnotize me and make me do silly things is put to rest when he explains how I'll remain in control and remember everything that happens. As he continues to give details on what we'll be doing and what our object is, I begin to get the feeling of excitement.

For the many years that I'd had an abiding faith in the Almighty's presence, I had seen first hand the many manifestations of God's miracles. I apparently still have a slight hope in my heart that there is a God watching over me. I wonder whether to be cynical of what Frank has in store for me or in awe of one of God's mysterious miracles.

I'm suddenly looking forward to this great adventure.

Chapter 23

     The counseling session with Frank has come to an end. I look at my watch and am amazed how quickly time has passed. Time seems to have stood still from the moment I sat down. It's almost three o'clock. I feel as though I'd just moments before sat down in Frank's office. He had begun by gently asking me questions, inviting me to remember things I'd long since forgotten. His gentle inquiries caused me to recall more and more from my past. I began to appreciate Frank's talents.

     At first, I remembered some silly decisions I'd made as a young adult in college. Then, with his calm prodding, Frank had me recalling events from my childhood. I began to recall other times in my life when I had, consciously or unconsciously, made life-altering decisions.

     I stand up when Frank stands and we both head for the hallway. I'm aware he's saying something as he leads me toward the front of the building but I'm not overly concerned with the objects in the hallway he's pointing out. My mind is more on the feeling of floating I'm experiencing, than on his words.

     This peaceful feeling began when I started talking in detail about the embarrassing running incident in the sixth grade. Frank continued to focus my attention on when I'd fallen flat on my face in the relay race, allowing me to recognize a decision I'd made while lying there, my blood from my scraped nose mixing with the dirt. As that young boy, I'd decide that it would hurt whenever I saw my body from a distance. So, I made very sure to never again become separated from my body. That decision has kept me from experiencing this feeling of rapture. Unlike my sixth grade catastrophe, this time I'm sure I'll not suddenly fall on my face. I suddenly realize another decision I had made that fateful day, lying face down on the track. I decided that running was not for me. Having made that decision, I have never again enjoyed the sport. I think I will like jogging now. With a smile, I realize Jim will appreciate my new attitude.

As amazed as I am with those realizations, what came next in my session with Frank astounds me even more. The thing that goes to the very heart of my current quandary concerning my faith.

One particular question Frank had asked brought to mind my sister's offer to drive me to my new parish. Before I knew it, I was telling Frank about leaving Detroit and coming to this town. I told him about the little car accident Maggie and I had been in. As I related the details, I began to recognize that, after having hit my head, I had lost consciousness for a short while. Amazingly, I then began to tell Frank what had occurred around me while I was unconscious. I recalled vividly the sounds of the surrounding traffic, the screeching of the tires, and the smell of the exhaust. I could almost see the crowd that had gathered around our wrecked cars. I could hear the voices of the crowd as they said such things as "are you okay" and "it's just a little accident." I especially recalled one woman's voice exclaiming, "There is no God!" The statement I had so taken into my heart and which had pushed aside my love for our Lord. The statement that has caused me six long months of grief.

After that revelation, I began to understand why I had felt so depressed. I finally understood where the voice in my head had come from. Any doubts I'd had about God, and His eternal love, has vanished.

I continue to float toward the front door feeling above it all and in total control. We reach the reception area where Frank picks up a business card from the desk. He turns his eyes toward me noticing my look of serenity. Smiling, he lightly grasps my arm and says, "How are you doing, Tommy?"

"Fine, thanks." My words are inadequate. True but inadequate. I am fine. Possibly I've never felt this fine in my life. Certainly not for a very long time. Maybe when I first fell in love with God, but not since then.

Thinking of God brings a bigger smile to my face. Seeing my smile broaden, Frank seems compelled to ask, "What's going on?"

"I was just thinking about what happened." I indicate the room we'd just left. "It's strange how that little car accident with my sister could have had such a huge effect on my beliefs. I hadn't even realized people were standing around talking. I knew I'd bumped my head pretty hard but I had no idea I was unconscious. And I certainly wasn't aware that anyone had said that there isn't a God." With disgust I add, "Why did I decide to believe her?" I shake off the unanswerable question. Then becoming curious I ask, "Does this occur often? That a person to recognizes the life-changing decisions they've made?"

Frank hands me the business card he'd picked up, then answers, "Very often. It's why I so enjoy doing this. Those of us who practice this procedure feel we're goofing off if we don't perform just this type of miracle each day." As the significance of his words hit me, he continues on a more mundane plane. "My phone number is on that card. Now that I've met Sandra's favorite priest, I'd very much like to stay in touch with you." We walk out of the building into the bright sunshine. "I'll drive you back to your church."

I feel like walking. Or floating. Or whatever I'm doing. With a silly smile on my face I say, "Thanks for the offer but I don't want to disturb this feeling by being enclosed in a car." I'm relieved when he isn't insulted and seems to understand my position. It's as though he's often heard the same thing expressed by others. Before leaving, I want to say something to show my appreciation, although I'm at a loss for words. I know something significant has happen to me. Something that has changed my outlook on life. I'm not quite sure I've figured it all out yet. Small revelations continued to occur to me. But I know one thing for certain. I owe my renewed love of our Lord, and my current feeling of invincibility to this man.

"Thank you," I say as I hold out my hand to shake his. "Thank you from the bottom of my heart."

He continues to smile as he returns my handshake. "Your welcome. Oh, and say 'Hi' to Sandra when you see her later this afternoon." He turns to reenter his office as he says. "And have a pleasant day." He walks back into the reception area as the door closes behind him.

His parting comment sets me to smiling broadly once again "I will. You can bet I will have a very pleasant day." I say to an already departed Frank.

I look at my watch to confirm that I'd been with Frank in his office for only an hour. Until Frank mentioned it, I'd forgotten about my six o'clock meeting with Sandra. I remember I must also call Jim and let him know we'd have to cancel our meeting since I'd be seeing Sandra this afternoon.

I find myself almost giggling with a childish sort of glee. I recognize all these worldly concerns I'd had in the past concerning time. With an inward smile, I realize, time is an easily overcome obstacle, given my present state of mind. The feeling of invincibility I'm experiencing seems to embrace time itself.

I still have to write this Sunday's sermon this afternoon. I mentally wave off any concern. I'll easily finish writing the sermon, and still make it on time to meet Sandra.

As I turn toward my church and start to walk, my mind goes over the many topics I can now include in sermons for the next few months. I wonder how my experience with Frank can be described to the skeptics who often are sitting in my pews on Sundays. My eyes have been opened to a totally new ways of helping my parishioners, and a new reason for them to have hope. I shan't forget that I too had been skeptical when Sandra and Frank first approached me with Frank's new procedure.

Along this line of being skeptical, a worthy topic for a sermon might be for one to leave their mind open to new ideas, because a miracle might be in the making. An open mind has enabled me to experience a miracle.

I have some doubt, though, whether my congregation will believe what I'd have to say about my day's adventure with Frank. If it hadn't happened to me, I'd not believe it either. I'm quite sure the hierarchy of The Church is not ready for such a jump from tradition. Hierarchies change slowly. An organization believing that sainthood is attained by the performance of one miracle in a lifetime is not ready for Frank's standard of a miracle a day.

Maybe if I take baby steps. Telling my story over many different Sundays, I can convince my congregation that daily miracles can be the norm. Maybe God has determined that the time has come to shake up the hierarchy of The Church.

Or maybe I'd write a sermon about my current feeling of rapture. My feeling of invincibility and serenity. I'm convinced joggers know it, as "being in the zone". Having been given a name, it must be more common than I'd formerly believed. And apparently there are many ways to achieve the feeling. My friend Jim achieves it by jogging. I achieved it by trying Mr. Hubbard's technique.

Unfortunately, such a sermon will only touch the hearts of those few athletes in my congregation. Or anyone lucky enough to have read the Dianetics book I'd been given, or met someone like Frank. It is also a topic I'll have to approach slowly over many sermons. I don't want to lose my audience because of their disbelief. As today has proven, faith is fragile, without God's intervening with an actual miraculous event.

I realize God has been leading me, these last few months, slowly and deliberately toward Frank's door. The theme of this week's sermon begins to take shape. Many times today I've wondered about God and His ways and how we mortals think of Him. Ramón suggested I must never forget the power of God. For me, today has been one of God's miracles. Today I've seen God's power and again been shown that He does indeed, work in mysterious ways. For me, today has been one of God's miracles. The theme of my next sermon will be the many mysterious ways in which God works. I will endeavor to get my parishioners to reevaluate the things that have happened in their own lives. My own experience will show them that, by taking the Lord into their hearts, they will be shown one of God's miracles. They too, might experience something wonderful.

I ponder the things that have happened to me today. A miracle happening without me fully realizing it. My short-lived break with God has been resolved. No doubt lingers in my mind. I love God with all my heart. The Devil has been exorcised.

The enormity of this fact causes tears to form in my eyes. I'd lost God's love for only six months, yet it seemed an eternity. I had missed my love of God. How would I have lived a lifetime without Him?

I will write a sermon pleading that my parishioners do as I did. Put their doubts aside. By opening my mind to a new idea, I gave Frank the opportunity to produce his miracle for today. A miracle that can only be the work of God. I can show my flock that a journey that began with a nice young lady's suggestion that I talk to her friend Frank. That the resurgence of my faith was brought to me by an unlikely messenger. Not by the teaching of a passing monk, or through the power of the Pope. But by a unique man with an unusual talent. That God had chosen Frank to be His messenger.

By having an acceptance toward another belief, and by opening my mind to a new idea, I got to see how God works. I've often been saddened that tolerance is frequently missing in our Christian faith. As Ramón had said earlier today, "God provides many routes into His Kingdom." Without tolerance and an open mind, we all will miss much, and I would have missed my miracle.

The half-mile walk to my church goes quickly. Upon entering the building, I see my dear friend and mentor, Ramón. He apparently notices the change in my demeanor, and my serene smile. It seems I've taken him by surprise.

"Hi, my boy. By the looks of you, I'd say you've had a very successful afternoon," He says with a curious look.

I wonder if I should tell him of my experience. He probably thinks my happiness has to do with meeting Sandra for lunch. Ramón comes from the old school of Catholicism so I'm concerned about his reaction to my afternoon's adventure. Nevertheless, I put my reluctance aside and take his earlier advice. I go with what's in my heart. He's undoubtedly noticed I have an all-encompassing smile on my face. How can I explain how silly it all was that I'd lost my love for God? And how it came about that I discovered the absurd truth?

I begin to chuckle. "I've had a wonderful afternoon. A miraculous thing has occurred. Do you have a minute? I'll tell you all about it."

Chapter 24

Ramón nods, giving me the time I ask for. His ever-present smile is in place, but his curiosity is obvious. We sit on the same pew where he had earlier told me to follow my heart, wherever it might lead. When he gave that advice I wonder if he'd assumed God would only work through the hands of a Catholic. Had Ramón even considered the possibility that God might also employ the hands of a non-Catholic? I'll trust his intelligence and compassion.

"I met an amazing man today, with an amazing talent," I say. I look into my Monsignor's eyes to see if he is receptive to what I had to say. "He has an unusual talent. A talent I would never have expected. In a very short time, he enabled me to recall a couple of traumatic moments in my past."

Ramón continues to watch me with rapt attention. I decide to continue. "More important than the traumas themselves were the decisions I made during those traumas. It was those decisions that have been raising havoc with my life. Making me conclude that Hell can actually be right here on Earth."

His smile broadens, a smile showing not only understanding but also anticipation for what is to come. He nods his head for me to continue.

"As luck would have it, the source of my biggest loss, my break from God, didn't lie very deep." As I relate my story, I can't stop smiling. How silly had been my demise.

"It all began with that little car wreck Maggie and I had while driving from Detroit." As I continue to tell Ramón about my afternoon of discovery, the depth of his understanding amazes me. "Frank is the man I've been with this afternoon. I knew I had hit my head but hadn't realized how hard. His technique actually had me remembering things I had overheard when I was unconscious." Knowing how impossible this might seem, I look to see how Ramón is responding to my tale. I'm gratified to see complete acceptance of my story. "One woman in the crowd had shouted out that there is no God. And I believed her. So, I decided to stop loving God, having been told that there is no God."

I chuckle at the absurdity of life as I continue, "That was the source of these many months of doubt. Such a small thing, yet so devastating to my life. The voice that kept going round and round in my mind saying 'There is no God' was that woman's voice. A woman, apparently in her distress seeing me bleeding. Not at all the voice one would expect from God. Or even from the Devil." I say smiling

Ramón is not at all surprised that a non-Catholic helped me re-acquire my love for God. He apparently already knows, as I had just learned this afternoon, that God's wonders are not restricted to Catholics. We both agree that God is not partial just to those in our faith.

I smile as he eloquently sums up my thoughts. "It's been my ongoing joy in life to observe the many different ways in which God performs His miracles. That's why I have always told my flock each Sunday to take God into their heart. It's why I told you this morning to follow your heart. By doing so, you'll be following God."

His words bring tears to my eyes. Today has been blessed. Early this morning, my dear friend Jim had promised a magical day is possible. And this wonderful man had predicted a few hours ago, that, by following my heart, I would give God an opportunity to work His miracles. I have lived the magic. The miracle.

Ramón pats me on the shoulder and then uses my body as a crutch to help him to his feet. He says, "I shan't be keeping you any longer. You told me you had a sermon yet to write and a meeting with the young lady yet to keep. And, I have a nap yet to take." He smiles broadly, then chuckles. As he walks away, I hear him say, "I get such a kick out of God and the nifty way He does

His stuff." If he weren't so ill, I think he'd be clicking his heels. He turns the corner and walks from my sight.

I check the time and realize I must hurry if I want to put my thoughts on paper for this week's sermon. I quickly walk to my office. Before starting my sermon, I call Jim's office and leave a message that I will have to cancel our afternoon meeting. Although I have many wonderful things to tell my friend, I'm glad to leave a message rather than try explaining in such a short time what I find almost inexplicable. The explanation will have to wait for another day of jogging, I decide.

Setting the phone down, I take pen in hand and began to write. My hand moves as though controlled by a higher force. I write furiously about the miracles of God. I use Monsignor Ramón's words about the importance of taking God into our hearts but I add my own slant to his ideas. Following one's heart is the path that allows God's will. It is the path we all must travel to reach the miracle that is Heaven. The miracle that must encompass us all. But, following our heart requires an open mind and tolerance for others.

Following my heart is exactly what I've done today. I took a chance and tried something new. And something miraculous occurred. Somehow, through this sermon and others to follow, I have to bring each member of my congregation to open his or her mind to new ideas, and to have a tolerance for the beliefs of others.

In a matter of minutes, I've written one of my best sermons. I've never felt so wonderful, so alive, and so able to confront life and all it's challenges. All this transformation in one short day. A day I'll never forget.

With satisfaction, I set my just finished sermon aside. Realizing that I'd better hurry to meet Sandra. For a day that had started with me in a sour mood, my current feeling is a need to be quirky. And, a need to run. The fact that I'm looking forward to jogging is a miracle in it's own right. Maybe I should wear those sweats my sister Maggie gave me for Christmas a couple years back. She was hoping to get me to take up some form of exercise.

If I jog over to the restaurant, I'll make it in time. I leave my office and head toward the rectory. How appropriate it will be to meet Sandra in jogging clothes, indicating my need to run off some of the excess energy I feel. After the fool I made of myself when we were suppose to be exercising this morning, my jogging to meet her will show her one of the more mundane results from my meeting with Frank.

Entering my room, I grin as I don my running pants. I quickly lace up and tie my shoes and head out toward the sunlight. If I continue to move this quickly, I'll arrive early at Satan's Cathedral for my rendezvous with Sandra. That's only fitting, since I was so late meeting her for lunch. I reach the sidewalk, turn left, and start to jog.

Crossing the street, I again see the park where I met up with Sandra this morning. My love for God knows no bounds. It was His voice telling her about my loss of faith and His hand that led me to Frank. I see now that my telling her about my loss was His work. How else would she have known to introduce me to Frank? How else would I have been allowed to remember those silly decisions that were so affecting my life?

As I jogged past the park, I pondered again my lame attempt at running when I'd been in the sixth grade, chuckling again over that ridiculous decision I'd made while lying with my face in the dirt and my nose feeling crushed. By deciding that running hurt too much, I had taken a very enjoyable pastime from my life. Laughing out loud, I picked up speed and felt the wind on my face. People can be so silly. So funny in their peculiarities. And so in need of help.

I see now that most people's lives are affected by the harmful decisions they've made in the past. But, God has given us a way to prevent those hapless decisions from continuing their destruction. The spread of Mr. Hubbard's techniques are a sorely needed tool in a chaotic world.

Apparently, my moving to this town was not happenstance. In God's plan, I am apparently His messenger. I must find a way to combine God's love with these new techniques. All I need do is follow my heart. God will show me the way.

As I near the restaurant, I slow to a trot, then a walk. I don't even feel winded and I haven't broken a sweat. Jogging is fun. I think I'll call Jim and tell him we should go jogging in the morning. Laughing, I realize how shocked he'll be by such a call from me.

After entering the restaurant, I find a seat and order a glass of water. My mind continues to relive today's events, from my early morning fight with exercise to my late afternoon experience with Frank. I'm so very thankful that I once again have the warm comfort of God's love in my heart.

I see Sandra entering the restaurant and gave her a wave. What a wonderful person she is. She helped me to find the way when I was so very lost.

Epilogue

Sandra

Six months later

As I enter Father O'Malley's church for the first time in six months, I realize how long it's been since I've been here, and how long it's been since I've seen him. I'm anxious to see how he's possibly changed. Many things have changed in all our lives since that day when the two of us had lunch with my friend Frank. I've heard wonderful things about how quickly Tommy's congregation has been growing since he took over, now that Monsignor Ramón is no longer with us.

Since that day six months before, I've resolved the conflict I had of knowing Tommy both as the man, and also as Father O'Malley the priest. I'm thankful that for a few short hours I got to know the man. But, now I want to see Father O'Malley, the priest, and see for myself how he is.

I've been putting off my visit back to his church, but this morning, I resolved I'd come and see how he is doing. With that in mind, I dressed in my Sunday best, and set out to do once more what I've gotten out of the habit of doing. I came to Mass

I choose a pew near the rear of the church, and remember back to when I'd first heard about Father O'Malley. It was well known in our town that Monsignor Ramón had terminal cancer, and that the Church's hierarchy was looking for a suitable replacement. The search for a replacement soon centered on newspaper stories about an exciting young priest who was doing so much good in the slums of Detroit. These articles inevitably centered on how filled with love he was. He had the reputation that, with love alone, he would be able to right anything wrong in the world.

At the time I became curious about what such a man might be like, so I started coming to Mass. That first time, I'd been uncomfortable being back in this church, even though I had loved the beautiful cathedral during my childhood visits. As a child I'd always loved walking into this exquisite church, with it's beautiful stain glass windows and the statuary and artifacts on the alter. I had customarily left the sanctuary of this building with a feeling of serenity flowing over me. Nevertheless as I grew older I got out of the habit of coming here.

That day about a year ago when I entered the sanctity of this cathedral after so many years of absence, I was once again impressed by its tranquility. I felt guilty that my reason for being here had been curiosity and not Christianity.

And then Father O'Malley entered the nave. The excitement from experiencing the beauty of this old building was eclipsed by the entrance of the young priest. He commanded everyone's attention as he walked in, his blue robe flowing behind him.

He took my breath away. I'd never seen such a beautiful man, with his wavy dark hair and those broad shoulders that even his priestly robe could not hide. I was immediately smitten, and have had a crush on him from that day forth.

I successfully ignored my childhood training that forbade sexual thoughts about priests. I'm certain that my years of religious backsliding contributed to my breech of Catholic customs. My mother would be mortified if she knew I'd looked at a priest with lust in my heart. I smile now as I recall how strongly I'd fallen for this forbidden man. If God found fault with my lusty feelings, I'm sure He has since forgiven me my transgressions. After all, it was I who set Tommy on the road to redemption. I was the one that introduced him to Frank.

For the next six months, I never missed a Sunday mass. Such had been my infatuation for the new priest. I flirted with him incessantly, sitting in a front pew and smiling at his every word. Never missing an opportunity to stand near him and talk with him at the end of the Service. I even started jogging in the park near his church, hoping one day we'd accidentally meet. When our chance meeting finally happened I was so excited I could hardly breath.

Introducing the man of my dreams to my friend Frank was as hard as anything I've ever done. I controlled my own urges and put Tommy's feelings before mine. What won the day was that childish habit of mine of trying to fix broken things. My parents were always chiding me for bringing home broken toys or injured animals. I see now my desire to help Tommy was only the same silly habit of wanting to fix something that was broken. Healing him had been more important than my giving into my own feeling of infatuation.

After introducing Tommy to Frank, I hung around just long enough to make sure they would get along. I also wanted to make sure I'd get to see Tommy later that so I could see firsthand how his session with Frank went. So, before leaving, I set up a tryst for drinks and dining. I didn't know whether I'd be meeting with a future lover. Or a dear friend.

I had gone to the bar with mixed feelings of excitement and terror, the result of the dichotomy I found myself in. On the one side, my fanciful romantic notion had come true. I realized Tommy had become attracted to me as a woman. With some shame, I've often thought that he didn't have a chance, what with the enticing way I'd acted in his Church. But, on the other side, Tommy had a lifelong and deep-seated love of God and Church. I'm not sure I could have lived with myself if I'd stolen him from God. So I figured if Tommy was still interested in me after meeting with Frank, at least I would have tried, and it wouldn't have been me that caused his renunciation. My gain. The Church's loss.

I thought that handing him over to Frank's care was a long shot. I should have realized that what Frank had done for me, he could easily repeat with Tommy. I knew when I left them that Tommy and Frank would spend some time together. Despite Tommy's insistence that his loss was nothing like my father's death, Frank coolly convinced him that there was a possibility that his sadness could be resolved. Frank and I were in silent agreement that Father O'Malley's loss of faith was certainly affecting him and any future life he might lead.

Later that day when I walked into the bar, I saw Tommy already sitting at a table. He had such a serene smile on his face and what I took as God's love shining brightly in his eyes. I knew immediately I'd made the right decision. The proper decision for

The Church and for Father O'Malley. And now I realize, it was even the right decision for me.

At the time, I wondered if I had sacrificed my own happiness. I tried not to show my heavy heart as I approached the table where Tommy was sitting. He was sipping from a glass of water, his eyes filled with the beautiful glow of love. He noticed me approaching his table and stood to offer his hand. I don't think he even noticed that the conspiratorial hugs and light kissing we'd done earlier in the day were missing. It was apparent that something had changed since early afternoon. This man was in love and it wasn't with me.

Now, six months after that sad ending to my romantic fantasy, I silently wait for mass to start. Looking around the beautiful cathedral, I see that most pews have filled.
Then, just as he had when I first set eyes on him a year ago, Father O'Malley steps through a side door and walks to the pulpit. He is again wearing a beautiful blue robe. As he leads us in the familiar rituals of the Mass, my mind wanders back to that dinner date six months ago when Tommy told me about his afternoon adventure with Frank. He knew he had ceased to believe in God but hadn't realized it was because of the voice in his mind telling him what to think. His happiness was apparent as he explained to me, "How could I continue to love God, if there was no God?"

When Tommy told me what he and Frank had done, I realized it was exactly the same technique Frank had used with me when he got me to remember my own ridiculous childhood decision. The decision I'd made that only my dad could bring me happiness. It was that pronouncement that had caused me such grief upon my dad's death. How devastating our childhood decisions can be later in life.

As Frank had done with me, he also did with Tommy, helping him to remember an incident that had been forgotten. Tommy had no memory of hitting his head in a car wreck. The ongoing effects he'd had were the recurring ache where his head had hit. The headache and, of course, the voice telling him that there is no God. Apparently the devil had been having his fun by damaging a priest's beliefs. With Frank's training of L. Ron

Hubbard's technique, Tommy relived the accident allowing him to dispel the effect of those words on him.

I again look toward the pulpit at the priest in front of me. His eyes are shimmering with a love I could never fulfill. His happiness is apparent. I again realize I did the right thing by introducing Tommy to Frank. It enabled Tommy to find the source of his loss of faith. That knowledge brought a complete resurgence of his abiding love of God and an accompanying resurgence in his dedication to The Church.

I wonder whether Frank and I were only messengers in a much larger saga. I wonder if my infatuation with Tommy and our chance meeting while jogging had been preordained. Maybe it had all been God's way of saving an exceptional priest for The Church. Or possibly I've yet to understand God's plan. Perhaps God does work in mysterious ways. Maybe in his mysterious way, God has given us all a tool to successfully exorcise the Devil. Once and for all.

Having witnessed what I came to see, I get up and quietly exit the church. I walk into the sunlight and look across the street to the park where I now jog most mornings. I smile as I think about the guy I met yesterday as I was jogging. Bob was moaning and groaning about how difficult it is to exercise and how horrible it is to jog.

Grinning, I recognize that some things in life keep happening in similar ways. I'm going to be having lunch with Bob this afternoon. I'll try to convince him that jogging can be fun. He has such sad and sorrowful eyes.

Smiling inwardly, I realize I still have the need to fix broken things. I've thought that maybe I should talk to Frank about that. I think not. Fixing broken things is one of my precious gifts.

Just look at Tommy.

Acknowledgment

L. Ron Hubbard, humanitarian, philosopher and author of "Dianetics, The Modern Science of Mental Health". The book, which inspired this story.

The following are trademarks and services marks owned by Religious Technology Center, Los Angeles, California, USA. These marks are licensed for use by the Church of Scientology International and its affiliated organizations and have been registered in many countries of the world.

CELEBRITY CENTRE, DIANETICS, HUBBARD, L. RON HUBBARD, L. RON HUBBARD signature, PURIFICATION, PURIFICATION RUNDOWN, SCIENTOLOGY, THE BRIDGE, DIANETICS symbol, SCIENTOLOGY cross (pointed), SCIENTOLOGY cross (rounded), SCIENTOLOGY symbol, VOLUNTEER MINISTER symbol, CHURCH OF SCIENTOLOGY OF NEW YORK logo.

SCIENTOLOGIST is a collective membership mark designating members of the affiliated churches and missions of Scientology.

APPLIED SCHOLASTICS and **NARCONON** are trademarks and service marks owned by the Association for Better Living and Education, Los Angeles, California, USA.

THE WAY TO HAPPINESS is a trademark owned by L. Ron Hubbard Library in the USA and in other countries.

www.ingramcontent.com/pod-product-compliance
Lightning Source LLC
Chambersburg PA
CBHW032005040426
42448CB00006B/492